NEW DIRECTIONS
FOR HIGHER EDUCATION

Number 33 • 1981

NEW DIRECTIONS
FOR HIGHER EDUCATION

A Quarterly Sourcebook
JB Lon Hefferlin, Editor-in-Chief
Martin Kramer, Consulting Editor

Number 33, 1981

Professional Ethics in University Administration

Ronald H. Stein
M. Carlota Baca
Guest Editors

Jossey-Bass Inc., Publishers
San Francisco • Washington • London

PROFESSIONAL ETHICS IN UNIVERSITY ADMINISTRATION
New Directions for Higher Education
Volume IX, Number 1, 1981
    Ronald H. Stein, M. Carlota Baca, Guest Editors

Copyright © 1981 by Jossey-Bass Inc., Publishers
                and
                Jossey-Bass Limited

New Directions for Higher Education (publication number
USPS 990-880) is published quarterly by Jossey-Bass Inc., Publishers.
Subscriptions are available at the regular rate for institutions,
libraries, and agencies of $30 for one year. Individuals may
subscribe at the special professional rate of $18 for one year.
New Directions is numbered sequentially—please order extra
copies by sequential number. The volume and issue numbers
above are included for the convenience of libraries. Second-class
postage rates paid at San Francisco, California, and at
additional mailing offices.

Correspondence:
Subscriptions, single-issue orders, change of address notices,
undelivered copies, and other correspondence should be sent to
New Directions Subscriptions, Jossey-Bass Inc., Publishers,
433 California Street, San Francisco, California 94104.

Editorial correspondence should be sent to the Editor-in-Chief,
JB Lon Hefferlin, at the same address.

Library of Congress Catalogue Card Number LC 80-84278
International Standard Serial Number ISSN 0271-0560
International Standard Book Number ISBN 87589-831-9

Cover design by Willi Baum
Manufactured in the United States of America

Contents

Editors' Notes

It is not too surprising that, during the past decade of consumer action, post-Watergate scruples, Abscam investigations, and cheating scandals from West Point to the Boston Marathon, our scrutiny should turn increasingly to the question of ethics. It is not very puzzling, either, that medical education has shown a growing concern for including humanities and ethics in its curriculum as a way of providing some guidance for the weighty decisions that life-sustaining technology does and will force upon us.

Ethics has long been the implied basis of most civilized and organized human activity. It is at the core of the often long-winded and lofty prose that makes up the codes of conduct for professionals and groups as disparate as physicians and Cub Scouts, the Secret Service, and social fraternities. There is one area of human endeavor where the concept of ethics is, perhaps, most inherent: education. Nowhere was ethics probed more than in the centers of learning of Greek antiquity, the universities of the Italian Renaissance, and eighteenth-century France. Ethics is again today a topic of concern and growing discussion, particularly on the campuses of colleges and universities.

Ethics has always prodded the collective conscience of higher education administration, but, in the heady affluence of the fairly recent past, it was relatively easy to be ethical. We were blessed by resources that permitted us to take risks, to make mistakes, and, perhaps most convenient, to cover those mistakes; one did not concern oneself too much about ethics in any formalized fashion. Administration was easier when there were fewer hard choices to make and the relative lack of crises provoked fewer ethical dilemmas. Now, of course, higher education administrators find—along with physicians, lawyers, and judges—that their profession has become terribly complicated. There are hard choices and little else. Today's academic vice-president must walk a tightrope between tenure recommendations, enrollment crises, high-demand vocational programs, and honest recruitment practices; college recruiters must balance the need for warm bodies against the need for maintaining academic quality.

This issue of *New Directions for Higher Education* contains chapters that have, in most respects, a direct bearing on the day-to-day responsibilities confronting administrators in their dealings with faculty, students, external regulators, and each other. Charles Chambers opens this sourcebook with a penetrating look at the bases of ethical responsibility and the social and philosophical history that has shaped our current understanding of intellectual morality in higher education. Of particular interest to any campus administrator, particularly those at or near the executive level, will be Donald Walker's chapter on ethical leadership and his enlightening descriptions of the "sacerdotal" and "secular" models of administrative style. The next three chapters deal with specific ethical dilemmas, which come about because someone, somewhere, has been abused. The first of the three is by Susan M. Vance, who writes on sexual harassment, a topic of special timeliness, given the fact that in April 1980 the United States Equal Employment Opportunity Commission issued interim guidelines defining illegal sexual harassment. The second, by Edward B. Fiske of *The New York Times*, concerns ethical practices in student recruitment. Finally, Paul Zuber has contributed a chapter on the obligations of predominantly white colleges and universities to their minority students. In the next two chapters, Elaine El-Khawas looks at self-regulation as one highly recommended method of assuring ethical practice in higher education, and John Farago examines self-regulation among administrators in light of the conflicts of interest that inevitably arise from the nature of the profession and the profession's clientele. We have also reproduced two basic policy statements regarding academic ethics, one from the American Association of University Professors concerning professional ethics, and the other from the American Association of University Administrators regarding professional standards for college and university administrators.

All but one of the chapters written for this sourcebook were originally presented at the ninth National Assembly of the American Association of University Administrators (AAUA), held in Toronto in June 1980. Increasingly aware of the hard choices facing academic institutions and the ethical quandaries that they provoke, the AAUA turned over the major portion of this assembly to a close investigation of ethical considerations in the administration of higher education. AAUA's interest in this theme, however, substantially predates the assembly: In 1975, AAUA adopted its code of professional rights and responsibilities, included in this volume, and it also provides a mediation service designed to help all higher education institutions and administrators uphold the principles articulated by these standards (see Hollander, 1980).

The assembly brought together men and women in the profession who had devoted considerable thought to these problems, and who had prepared some philosophical (and, indeed, very practical) approaches to the quest for solutions. From the outset, the assembly agreed that, as long as there are institutions where debate flourishes, where certain groups have more influence or power over others, where there are internal bureaucracies and external pressures, and where the many constituencies represent the whole social body, there will, indeed, be ethical problems that would drive even Solomon to convene a committee.

The idea of devoting a national conference and an issue of *New Directions for Higher Education* to the theme of the role of ethics in higher education administration belongs to Charles Chambers of the Council on Postsecondary Accreditation. We are indebted to Dr. Chambers, not only for contributing the opening chapter to this sourcebook, but also for substantially developing its theme. We would like to express our appreciation to the American Association of University Administrators, its board, and its president, Father Edmund Ryan, for their cooperation in the preparation and sponsorship of this sourcebook. We also thank Judy Zuckerman for her editorial assistance, and Martha Fiorella and Mary Quirk for their typing skills, patience, and good humor.

M. Carlota Baca
Ronald H. Stein
Editors

Reference

Hollander, P. A. "A Mediation Service for Administrators Regarding AAUA Standards." In J. E. McCarthy (Ed.), *New Directions for Higher Education: Resolving Conflict in Higher Education*, no. 31. San Francisco: Jossey-Bass, 1980.

M. Carlota Baca is an assistant to the president at the State University of New York at Buffalo and director of the University's Honors Program. She is a former American Council on Education Fellow and recently served as program co-chairperson of AAUA's National Assembly IX.

Ronald H. Stein is an assistant to the president at the State University of New York at Buffalo. He was program co-chairperson for the AAUA National Assembly IX, and is consulting editor for New Directions for Higher Education. *Stein has published articles on the topics of the impact of federal regulations on higher education and law and higher education.*

*Examines ethical behavior as an extension of our
legal doctrine. Academic freedom, in loco parentis,
and the charitable status of academic institutions are
basic sources of ethical responsibility for college and
university administrators.*

Foundations of Ethical Responsibility in Higher Education Administration

Charles M. Chambers

Ethical issues arise in all political, commercial, and social settings; neither are they confined to the last fourth of western civilization's twentieth century. Archaeological records from the early Mesopotamian cultures show duplicity by politicians, sharp dealing by merchants, and seduction by false teachers. Throughout history every civilized society has developed a framework of acceptable norms of behavior which, among other things, creates loyalty, coherence, and unity in the social order. However, during times of social stress and change, the stabilizing effect of traditionally established and broadly accepted moral convictions is lessened. Unless a special effort is made to maintain ethical responsibility, the esteem and confidence which our social institutions, such as higher education, enjoy will be threatened and, equally significantly, many trusting individuals will suffer abuse, exploitation, and the associated mental distress and anxiety, which may have everlasting effects.

While all professions that contain a large element of public confidence and trust face eroding values, nowhere has the ethical slope become more slippery than on our college and university campuses. The swinging sophistication of the 1970s has softened our vigilance; and, as we face the lean years of the 1980s, there will be growing incentives to cut corners. The combination of these two phenomena working in tandem greatly reinforces the need to review carefully the foundations of ethical responsibility in higher education at this time.

While there are universal statements of fundamental ethical principles which hold true in all settings, it is also accepted that they are notoriously useless in providing helpful guidance for practical problems. By examining the sources of moral behavior that arise in the academic setting, we can begin to understand how the general principles are to be applied. In particular, there are a number of unique aspects of higher education administration which have ethical consequences going beyond the normal levels of socially expected behavior.

The first aspect regards the nature of the clientele. Despite a gradu-ally increasing average age for college students, the fact remains that significant numbers of young persons get their first chance to learn about adult behavior on the college campus. Although they may appear mature, and even be legally classified as adults, most college students are still searching for their life goals and are steadily forming personal values and beliefs. Consequently, many students are susceptible to exploitation, abuse, manipulation, or simply neglect by college personnel who, despite the decline of the legal doctrine of *in loco parentis*, remain powerful role models for young minds.

A second, unique, aspect involves the autonomy in research and scholarship cherished by the higher education community. The values of academic freedom are founded upon free speech, professional objectivity, and peer collegiality. Indeed, the stock in trade of colleges and universities are ideas, and our nation has recognized that they are the most powerful social force known to man. To protect the integrity and vitality of the search for truth and its transmission and application as recorded knowledge, higher education has been given a most enviable degree of deference by government at the federal, state, and local levels. Further, the courts have spread the mantle of First Amendment protections widely across academia and, in the absence of a showing of arbitrariness or capriciousness, have generally accepted at face value the decisions of college faculty and administrators. Legislatures have passed many statutes expressly prohibiting their respective executive branches from intruding into the academic affairs of higher education.

A third aspect involves the special place which higher education shares with other groups in society as a charitable enterprise. The concept of charity. here is not so much one of contributing to the welfare of the needy, but rather relieving the government of work that would be much more burdensome for it to do by itself. In recognition of this service to society, our tax laws at all levels grant significant exemptions to higher education. These benefits, coupled with the billions of dollars of public funds directly expended on higher education, place higher education in the most respectful position of a public trust. While few college personnel take oaths as public officials, we all have obligations, first, not to abuse these privileges; and second, to apply our knowledge and skills to the well being of society.

In the subsequent sections of this chapter I will examine the nature of ethical behavior as a natural extension of legal doctrine in this country, including its philosophical and religious dimensions. We will then discuss in more detail how the three unique aspects of higher education, that is, *in loco parentis*, academic freedom, and charitable status, thoroughly justify the highest degree of attention to ethical matters by college officials.

Law and Ethics

The legal system of our country, as inherited from the British Common Law and developed through our numerous constitutions, is infused with ethical doctrine. Indeed, any society that can boast of stable governance will have a very close relationship between its legal authority and its moral beliefs. The German philosopher, Georg Jellinek (1878), has defined law as the "ethical minimum" to reflect the fact that certain basic beliefs of moral behavior are so necessary to the continued functioning of society that the government institutes strict processes to guarantee compliance. Ultimately, the sanctions involve the physical power of the sovereign to control offenders. Yet, even in this view, it is not possible to segregate the legal mandates from the ethical norms; because, in the final analysis, the sovereign only has enforcement power to the extent that the citizens at large concur in the ethical "rightness" of the laws and are willing to obey them. It is noted by Solomon Freehof (1953) that: "Police power is, of course, essential, yet never quite sufficient. If a large percentage of the citizens decided to be violent, as has happened repeatedly, the police power is helpless. The true source of order comes from within. It is conscience which makes citizens of us all."

The law can be thought of as that subpart of ethical practice which the society, in its wisdom, has decided is so essential to survival as to require coercion to maintain. Even though the exact dividing line between unethical and illegal practices may be somewhat gray, there are basic criminal activities in our country that the law considers patently illegal. Some examples of "white collar" crimes to which college administrators should be alert are: larceny/embezzlement, bribery, assault/battery, discrimination, libel/slander, and malfeasance. Thus, it is not surprising to find within the law many elements of ethics, such as motive, intent, desire, manipulation, conflict of interest, deceit, disloyalty, abuse of advantage, and exploitation of opportunity. Consequently, there is no sharp dividing line between legal and ethical principles and indeed the line shifts from one direction to the other as the government redefines those matters of social comport which it considers absolutely necessary. For example, many local jurisdictions adopted "blue laws" early in our history to regulate commerce on Sunday. A person with different moral or religious beliefs had no choice but to accept the inconvenience. However, as society has moved toward a less parochial role for government in overseeing how we use our time, many such regulations have been abolished. As this line has shifted, a person's shopping habits are now more a matter of personal ethical convictions than law.

The immediate consequence of this relationship is that an illegal act is, within the context of the given society, an unethical act. Claims that it may be in some instances morally correct to disobey the law must be based on a code of ethical or religious convictions such as "human law" which is broader than that held by the society. In our country especially, full provision is made within the legal system for redress of all grievances.

Next, it is true that the only ethical behavior which a society can demand from one of its members is that which is codified as a legal obligation. As explained by Edgar Bodenheimer (1962) in *Jurisprudence:* "[N]o one is required to play the part of a good Samaritan and bind up the wounds of a stranger who is bleeding to death, or to cry a warning to one who is walking into the jaws of a dangerous machine" (p. 95). Indeed one has a legal right *not* to be gracious or charitable in the sense that, for example, should he be harassed by others to give to the poor, he may obtain a court injunction against those others to protect his privacy.

However, as will be discussed later, there are many reasons for society to expect the highest ethical behavior from certain persons who have been entrusted with the public interest. Thus the amoral person, who obeys only the law but nothing more, may never be convicted, but will also never gain the trust and respect of the community.

Further, even if a person is not motivated by conscience to meet a higher level of morality than required by the law, one should be motivated by self-interest. In this country, society has endorsed the concept of self-regulation in the learned professions, in which higher education is typically included. Such self-regulation normally operates through both formal and informal Codes of Good Practice by which peers judge acceptable performance of their colleagues. Such codes are based almost exclusively on ethical principles and it is well established that when such privileged groups fail to uphold the accepted ethical norms, society moves rapidly to expand the legal system to make compliance with the principles mandatory. This regulation represents a reduction in personal liberty and an expansion of government that contradicts the faith in the individual on which the United States was founded.

Given this relationship between law and ethics, let us now turn to the nature and function of ethical principles themselves. There are two traditional sources of morality. The first is based on the inner conscience of man as a rational being who will act from a sense of duty to do good for its own sake. As expressed by Julius Moor (1922), man will adhere to moral norms because of "the inner conviction of their inherent rightness." The foundations of a complex philosophical system that reflects both the potentials and frailties of human nature was laid by Aristotle and has continued to the modern day through what might generally be termed *natural law*.

The second is a belief in revelation from God about how man should use his free will and intellect. While many contributions to ethical thought are found in the non-western cultures such as Moslem, Hindu, and Buddhist, our country has inherited in large measure a Judeo-Christian tradition based on the Old and New Testaments and which has been interpreted for guidance of human affairs by the organized religions. Such a focus reflects an existing cultural tradition in this country that infuses not only our laws but also our social institutions, such as health, welfare, and education.

We may conclude therefore that either in goodness or grace people will want to do what is right. Yet any consideration of ethical principles eventually arrives at a point of trying to define what is "right" or "good" or "moral" or "proper" or "correct." Of course, there is no applicable dictionary entry. On the one hand, there are those who insist on strict obedience to religious doctrine; that is, the "thou shalls" and the "thou shall nots." On the other hand, there are those who feel that ethics can be stretched to justify desired action in any situation; for example, "if it feels good—do it." A middle view stresses trying to achieve the greatest "good" while causing the least "harm." It should be clear that without some benchmark of what constitutes acceptable behavior it is possible to argue in favor of any position.

The difficulty is that ethics is not a well indexed code of behavior to be consulted when in doubt, but is rather a system of thought developed over many millennia about how human beings translate their inner motivations into external actions having social consequences. It is what makes civilizations civilized and is based upon cultural tradition and heritage. A person's ability to make ethical choices requires some basic perception of the history of civilizations and the image of man on which they were founded. Regardless of one's religious persuasion, it is true that the recorded scriptures first presented the vision of man as a moral being. Man then found within his own intellect justification for ethical behavior. As an indispensable aid to understanding ethics, let us briefly examine what it is about man that makes him want to know what is right and then do it.

The root of ethical obligations arising from either the natural law or the inspired scriptures is much the same. Both recognize man's ability to rationally exercise free will over the whole of nature and his fellow man. Of course, the intricate question of how "free" free will is can never be answered. Yet, there is enough certainty to the reality of man's dominion over a Nature he did not create but which was given to him to evoke ethical duties. This dominion has permitted him to organize societies and institutions within societies which genuinely support and improve the good of the order. It is clear then that man has been given something very precious in trust and has obligations, beyond merely surviving, to act as custodian, steward, prudent manager, and guardian of nature, which includes his fellow man. Even an atheistic society cannot ignore the fundamental self-interest served by nurturing its own human and natural resources.

As expressed in the First Chapter of Genesis in the Old Testament: "Then God said, Let us make man in our image, after our likeness: and let them have dominion over the fish of the sea, and over the fowl of the air, and over the cattle, and over all the earth, and over every creeping thing that creepeth upon the earth" (Gen. 1:26), and "God saw every thing that he had made and behold it was very good. . ." (Gen. 1:31). Man's "dominion" expresses his rationality, his free will, and his obligation of prudent stewardship. This central revelation, also found in other scriptures, can be taken as an ethical definition of good or right, that is, man's obligation is to use, without abuse, that which has been given him in nature.

In our country, it is reasonable to characterize the acceptable level of ethical behavior in terms of the moral doctrines of Christianity, which, of course, are found in the teachings of the Messiah, Jesus Christ. Indeed general Christian morality is ethically compatible with (if not the fulfillment of) the teachings of the Hebrew patriarchs, on which it is clearly based. Further, through an elaborate synthesis developed by St. Thomas Aquinas, the Christian teachings are found to have much in common with the ethical principles derived from the secular theory of natural law handed down from Aristotle. Let us now consider how behavior can indeed be judged to be ethical.

A very general approach for analyzing what is ethical behavior or what is proper stewardship is found in the concept of contract. A great deal of basic legal theory can be analyzed in terms of contracts, either between two individuals or between an individual and society at large. The basic elements of a contract are an agreement between the parties that each will fulfill certain obligations or honor certain duties in consideration of certain privileges or benefits offered by the other in exchange. Under the law, the terms of a properly formed contract, which may even be a citizen's obligation not to negligently harm other citizens, can be judicially enforced. In the ethical setting there is no direct enforcement but the same relationships between the parties can be examined and various duties defined which, when breached, indicate unethical behavior.

As in the law, the fairness of the ethical contract can be measured by such factors as one, the relative capacity of the parties to make an agreement; two, the properness of the kind of performances to be expected; and three, even unforeseen intervening circumstances that would make a breach of the contract less ethically culpable.

Let us examine two elements of contract which will be most important to developing the foundation of ethical responsibility within higher education. First, contract theory looks to the relative capacity of the parties to negotiate an arm's length agreement. It is assumed that if the parties are equal in strength then each is able to protect his own position and demand an appropriate performance from the other in exchange for the benefits he is offering. In such a situation of informed consent, neither party has any special obligations to the other to disclose all pertinent information relevant to the terms of the contract. Even white lies, which in Aristotle's view always remain "mean and culpable," can be tolerated if it appears that the parties have enough alertness and understanding of the situation to discount puffery or bluffing. However, when one of the parties is intrinsically more susceptible to persuasion and less able to separate fact from fable, then caution is urged. When the more sophisticated party creates misunderstandings, either intentionally or by omission, an imperfect contract is formed. It is then ethically improper for the senior party to demand that the other comply with all the terms. Further, when a party receives a great deal of consideration in a contract in the form of privileges, prerogatives, and rights, a fair contract requires that that party assume a commensurate level of obligations and duties to earn the benefits. Indeed even in the law a lopsided contract is called *unconscionable* and may not be enforced by the courts.

Having presented a general overview of the relationships between law and ethics, the sources of ethical responsibility and the requirements of a fair contract, let us now examine the unique factors in higher education which dictate the most sterling degree of ethical behavior.

In Loco Parentis **Revisited**

In 1913 a Kentucky court made the following statement about a college's relationship to its students: "College authorities stand in loco parentis concerning the physical and *moral* welfare and mental training of the pupils, and we are unable to see why, to that end, they may not make any rule or regulation for the government or betterment of their pupils than a parent could for the same purpose." (*Gott* v. *Berea College,* 161 S. W. 204, 206 (1913)) (emphasis added). Since that time this legal principle has been severely eroded by a series of cases expanding the individual rights and protections of students and a general lowering of the age of majority which, for legal purposes, makes adults of practically all college students. Yet, in terms of the ethical contract, college students remain very susceptible to the seductive sophistry of the college campus.

Thus, the parties to the college contract are very unbalanced, with one being quite vulnerable in terms of a sophisticated understanding of the promises made by the other and the other having an excessive amount of influence. This creates a great disparity between the parties requiring the utmost level of professionalism and ethical responsibility on the part of college officials. To meet this ethical obligation, an institution must not just be fair and accurate, but must add an extra measure of disclosure and explanation to ensure that students can intelligently consent to the contract. Nowhere else is this abyss between the relative bargaining power of the parties greater than perhaps in the health care industry. As explained earlier, such a situation requires a great degree of vigilance by the senior party to ensure that the junior party is not being exploited. Precautions that would appear extraordinary in a balanced bargaining situation may be necessary here to ensure ethical behavior.

Next, it is extremely unlikely that any college official has intentionally misled, seduced, or exploited a student without coating the relationship in a thick layer of intellectual rationalization. Given the fact that few of us are that good looking or charming, such academic chicanery can easily become a disreputable stock in trade. Further, such unethical behavior distorts and otherwise scandalizes the moral development of the students. The unconscionable nature of such a breach of integrity by college officials is reflected in the New Testament (Matt. 18:6, 7) where scandalizing children and leading young minds astray is portrayed as a most heinous offense.

It is beyond the scope of this chapter to explore ways that colleges can fulfill their ethical responsibilities. However, it should be clear that higher education officials have a vital ethical responsibility in dealing with their students. We must not forget that our students are exposed to an environment in which the dimensions of ambiguity and relativity in knowledge and its social meaning are intentionally explored. In such a context the student is expected to test his or her ethical assumptions, experience growth through scholarship, and learn to accept personal responsibility as the price of intellectual independence. The psychologist, Lawrence Kohlberg (1969), has studied the levels of mental development as a person's ethical perceptions mature. In the latter stages, frequently developed at the collegiate level, persons are able to accept and even initiate social change with an understanding of how the basic moral principles, on which the society is founded, are being preserved. As social institutions, our colleges and universities can have no more noble goal. Pursuit of knowledge is futile if there is not a stable, mature society supporting the academy and drawing wisdom from its springs.

In the next two sections we examine other sources of ethical obligations in higher education which would exist even if students were fully able to enter into arm's length contracts for their education. We note, however, that the nature of the contract changes somewhat in certain areas.

Academic Freedom

The area of academic freedom can also be examined in terms of contract principles, but they must be viewed somewhat more broadly than simply an agreement between two parties such as a student and an institution. In general, the ethical contract, which leads to moral obligations, is formed between collegiate personnel and the society at large, and thus is usually referred to as a *social contract*. The concept of a social contract, initially developed by the seventeenth-century philosophers Thomas Hobbes (1946) and Benedict Spinoza (1895), was a way to explain the need for societies to form governments that could translate the moral dictates of the natural law into rules of behavior to be enforced by law. Their theory was refined in the early eighteenth century by John Locke (1946) and Baron Charles Louis de Montesquieu (1900) so as to protect the liberty of the individual citizen. They proposed organizing the government into executive, legislative, and judicial branches, with each acting as a check and balance on the others.

The philosophical underpinnings of systems of government have taken many complex turns over the last two centuries. What can be concluded from this is that our legal system provides a stable social order permitting a high degree of individual intellectual expression. The social contract between society and its central institutions, such as education, can be examined to determine what rational basis exists for expecting certain levels of ethical behavior from individuals in certain privileged positions. Since much can be based on natural law, let us look briefly at nature in order to appreciate our legacy as educators.

In nature, propagation of species is accomplished by transmission of genetic information from one generation to the next. As particularly effective survival strategies are worked out by each species, they will be preserved generally to the extent that they have become instinctive in that species. The higher mammals, including early man, improved on this tedious and harsh process of natural selection by developing the social process of education. Parents would pass on to their offspring skills, competencies, and knowledge they had received from their parents and that likely had been embellished by their own experiences. This technique accelerated the cumulative effect of improved survival strategies for those groups willing to form societies and expend some effort in preparing the next generation, that is, teach them.

It may be that the urge to teach has become instinctive in some species, but it is clear that at least *what* is taught is based on individual experiences in the real world, for both man and animal. Clearly this is a much more efficient process than letting nature modify genetic information, since fresh understandings can be acquired, tested, and refined within a single generation. However, like instinct, such wisdom must be passed in its entirety from one generation to the next. Just as the amount of genetic information that can be passed between generations is limited, so is the amount of information an older member of a species can pass on to a younger member.

Next, man is unique among the known species in having been gifted with the ability to refine his communications through sophisticated speech patterns and to record them in physical forms which can survive, by many orders of magnitude, the life spans of the persons making the records. This generation-spanning strategy has enabled man to dramatically accelerate the achievement of his intellectual potential within a brief period of several thousand years by accumulating and refining the best wisdom each generation has to offer and preserving it for transmission to future generations. This strategy has, of course, enabled man to see much farther than all the other species combined by, in the words of Galileo, "standing on the shoulders of giants."

The obvious conclusion of this scenario is that the American higher education community has inherited a large part of this legacy and has developed an ethical and social framework for ensuring that the knowledge discovered and added to the reservoir meets the highest standards of objectivity and scholarship. Our society in particular has acknowledged this crucial role of higher education both in law and in practice and has endorsed the privileges of academic freedom, collegial governance, and tenure as necessary to ensure these benefits to society.

For its part in this social contract, the higher education community has an obligation to make certain that the highest levels of scholarship, objectivity, and recognition of merit distinguish all of its activities. For example, tenure is offered to an individual scholar so that he or she may pursue creative academic endeavors unfettered by external political and economic influences. An initial ethical obligation under such a contract is that a tenured faculty member indeed strives continually to be a productive scholar, and that evidence of failure to serve the discipline and the academy would be at least ethical grounds to expect the person to relinquish the professional chair. It should also be apparent that any treatment of students that is not compatible with the professional responsibilities of scholarship must be judged unethical.

Let us examine one social dilemma that is a consequence of this ethical formulation. Based on this discussion, one would have to agree that it is morally improper for higher education officials to grant recognition through degrees, certificates, credits, or even admissions, to persons who have not merited them through intellectual achievement. Yet, with the willing complicity of the higher education community, our society has adopted educational credentials as stepping stones to successful careers. Then, in an effort to assure equal opportunity and affirmative action for disadvantaged groups, society has called on our colleges and universities to open their doors wide.

Clearly it remains ethically improper, as a falsehood, to permit persons to think they have achieved something academically which they have not. To meet this ethical dilemma higher education has a duty to transmit more effectively the wealth of academic knowledge of which it acts as guardian. Individualized instruction is generally more expensive than the traditional classroom approach, but more may be needed in order to provide educational opportunities for disadvantaged individuals. At the same time, higher education can expect society to provide the increased resources to carry out this much more intensive and expensive format of education. It would be ethically improper for higher education officials to shrink from the challenge of educating the disadvantaged, but they should insist that they have an equally ethical responsibility to protect and nurture the values of the academy. If special formats are needed for some special clienteles, then a greater allocation of society's resources must be made to higher education.

Charitable Status

Another set of important privileges and benefits that higher education enjoys in this country is favorable treatment under tax laws at the federal, state, and local levels. This not only involves various exemptions and credits for virtually every tax category, such as real estate, inventory, sales, income, bequests, but also the opportunity to attract contributions from donors who thereby are permitted significant tax deductions. There are very few legal obligations which higher education must meet in order to obtain these benefits, the primary limitation being that none of the surplus revenues that may be produced can inure to private benefit.

Higher education receives these benefits under our tax laws because it is classified as a charitable enterprise. The term charity must be construed in the broad sense of serving the public interest and the government at large, rather than simply helping to improve the welfare of indigents. Rather, our country has recognized that colleges and universities, among others, add to social stability and foster the benefits of voluntarism and pluralism in America. Further, higher education is something that our government would provide on its own, if it had to. However, the existence of our autonomous colleges and universities relieves the government of the need to do so itself and therefore higher education is serving the public interest.

Further, since the traditional purpose of taxation is to produce revenue for the operation of government, it would be somewhat inconsistent to extract levies from organizations that are doing something the public needs (and probably at less expense than the government itself could do it). In a sense, higher education's tax benefits are nothing more than prudent and pragmatic tax policy. Indeed if the government inhibits such beneficial activities by taxation, it might find itself having to spend more than it collects to replace the services its levies have curtailed.

This perspective is important because higher education, among others, is frequently the target of charges that it lives on special tax preferences or "loopholes" and that, in reality, the government is "subsidizing" the enterprise through reverse appropriations, that is, it forgoes the opportunity to collect additional taxes. Only the most myopic advocate of big government for big government's sake would find this argument attractive.

Although not on the same grand scale of human existence as academic freedom, it should be clear that the charitable status enjoyed by colleges and universities is part of the social contract between higher education and the American public. Because public resources are involved, higher education holds this trust as a fiduciary and can be expected to exercise ethically sound judgment in serving the public interest.

Conclusion

The three fundamental sources of ethical responsibility discussed in this chapter—*in loco parentis*, academic freedom, and charitable status— are characteristic of higher education and go far beyond the general duties of citizenship. With this reaffirmation of the moral leadership to be exercised by college faculties and administrators, I hope that some attention will be paid to the more practical aspects of ethical behavior in higher education that are discussed in the subsequent chapters of this sourcebook.

References

Bodenheimer, E. *Jurisprudence, The Philosophy and Method of the Law*. Cambridge, Mass.: Harvard University Press, 1962.

Freehof, S. "The Natural Law in the Jewish Tradition." In *University of Notre Dame Natural Law Institute Proceedings*. Vol. 15. Notre Dame, Ind.: University of Notre Dame Press, 1953.

Hobbes, T. *Leviathan*. Oxford, England: Clarendon Press, 1946.

Jellinek, G. *Die Sozialethische Bedeutung von Recht, Unrecht, and Strafe*. Vienna: 1878.

Kohlberg, L. "Stage and Sequence: The Cognitive Developmental Approach to Socialization." In D. Goslin (Ed.), *Handbook of Socialization Theory and Research*. Chicago: Rand McNally, 1969.

Locke, J. *The Second Treatise of Government*. Oxford, England: Basil Blackwell, 1946.

Montesquieu, C. *The Spirit of the Laws.* New York: Hafner, 1900.
Moor, J. *Macht, Recht, Moral.* Szeged: 1922.
Spinoza, B. *Tractatus Theologico-Politicus.* London, England: 1895.

*Charles M. Chambers is currently vice president of
the Council on Postsecondary Accreditation, for
which he served as acting president during 1980. The
holder of a Ph.D. degree in Mathematical Physics and
a J.D. degree in Administrative Law, Chambers has
held faculty appointments at Harvard University, the
University of Alabama, and George Washington
University. He also has a Deanery appointment to the
Pastoral Council of the Roman Catholic Diocese
of Arlington, Virginia.*

*A campus president's task is to understand and
reconcile dichotomies between the perspectives of the
professional and manager.*

The President as Ethical
Leader of the Campus

Donald E. Walker

Certainly, it would be foolish to deny that the leader of an organization
influences and helps create the climate in which the organization will
transact its affairs. At the national level, we need only remember Watergate
to have that point brought home to us, although in a negative fashion.
Rather than talking about the obvious responsibilities of the president to
set a high ethical tone for the way in which administrators and faculty
members transact their business, however, I would rather talk about the
models of campuses we have in our heads and the derivative roles of campus
workers as sources of misunderstanding about ethical issues. To begin, let
me emphasize that truly unethical behavior, in the broadest and deepest
sense in which society understands that term, is rare in academic communities. There are certain standards of right and wrong behavior that are
fundamental to our campuses. No stable person would argue that falsify-
ing results of laboratory experiments is ethical; no one would argue that
selling grades for cash or favors is ethical behavior; and no one would argue
the morality of theft or embezzlement. All in all, we are a rather high-

I wish to acknowledge the great contribution in the formulation of this
chapter of Dr. David Feldman, dean, School of Business, U.S. International
University.

minded ethical bunch. Nevertheless, in times of stress, chronic and deep-seated mutual suspicions surface on the part of administrators and faculty, each group questioning the other's standards of conduct. One does not have to be around a campus long before these differing perspectives become obvious.

I recently attended a dinner in honor of a dean who had decided, after a number of years as a successful administrator, to return to the faculty. He said in the course of his remarks, "When I became a dean and crossed the campus to the administration building, I discovered that somewhere in the journey I had crossed a line that separated sons of bitches from other people, and I had become a son of a bitch. Now I propose to recross that line in the right direction." Another administrator once observed about the faculty, "I am continually amazed by how such principled men and women can rationalize being so totally unprincipled when their own self-interest is at stake." Such mutual suspicion, it seems to me, is rooted in differing interpretations of behavior, rather than in the behavior itself. The misunderstandings go back, on the one hand, to the dichotomy between professional and managerial perspectives, and, on the other, to the conflict between what we might call the *secular* and the *sacerdotal* views of the campus. To retreat to the old cliche, "Where you stand depends on where you sit." I suggest that it is the president's task to understand and reconcile this dichotomy.

Sources of Conflict Between Faculty and Administrators

The conflict between professional and managerial perspectives goes back to the problem of a democratic society: How can critical decisions rest with the people when those questions are to be decided in areas of specialization inhabited by experts? The populist point of view is expressed in the dictum "War is too important to be left to generals." To pose the conflict in the opposite perspective, "How can laymen possibly make judgments that could do anything but complicate the problems physicians have in conquering disease and treating patients?"

The bromidic answer that the professionals, the experts, will deal with the means and the people will determine the ends has not always worked. Society is obviously still adjudicating many such issues. These dilemmas come to the campus in the form of differing perceptions over the nature of authority. As Etzioni (1964) puts the matter, "The most basic principles of administrative authority and the most basic principle of authority based on knowledge—or professional authority—not only are not identical but they are quite incompatible" (p. 76). Etzioni continues this discussion by examining the difference between administrative and professional authority:

Administration assumes a power hierarchy. Without a clear ordering of higher and lower in rank, in which the higher in rank have more power than the lower ones and hence can control and coordinate the latter's activities, the basic principle of administration is violated; the organization ceases to be a coordinated tool. However, knowledge is largely an individual property; unlike other organization means, it cannot be transferred from one person to another by decree. Creativity is basically individual and can only to a very limited degree be ordered and coordinated by the superior in rank. Even the application of knowledge is basically an individual act, at least in the sense that the individual professional has the ultimate responsibility for his professional decision. The surgeon has to decide whether or not to operate. Students of the professions have pointed out that the autonomy granted to professionals who are basically responsible to their consciences (though they may be censured by their peers and in extreme cases by the courts) is necessary for effective professional work. Only if immune from ordinary social pressures and free to innovate, to experiment, to take risks without the usual social repercussions of failure, can a professional carry out his work effectively. It is this highly individualized principle which is diametrically opposed to the very essence of the organizational principle of control and coordination by superiors— that is, the principle of administrative authority. In other words, the ultimate justification for a professional act is that it is, to the best of the professional's knowledge, the *right* act. He might consult his colleagues before he acts, but the decision is his. If he errs, he still will be defended by his peers. The ultimate justification of an administrative act, however, is that it is in line with the organization's rules and regulations, and that it has been approved—directly or by implication—by a superior rank (p. 76).

Obviously, administrators fall on the power hierarchy side, and faculty members identify with the professional perspective. I shall return to this point shortly to discuss its implications for the perspective each group has on what is acceptable—that is, ethical—behavior and what is not. But first, let us look at the related matter of how the two groups view the nature of the university. I contend that the faculty not only holds this professional perspective of their own activities, but that they also view the university as sacerdotal, while administrators tend to hold a secular view.

The Sacerdotal View

First, let me describe the sacerdotal, or professional, view of the campus. I emphasize that this is a perception of how the campus ought to work, an ideal type. Even the most ardent and stereotyped member of the most traditional faculty would not maintain that the campus usually or ever actually operates like this; it is merely that it should. This point of view begins with the question of the nature of knowledge. Knowledge and learning are for mankind and for the ages. Ultimately, of course, knowledge is valued because it is useful to human beings. Sometimes, however it takes many years or even centuries to see the ways in which that information can be used or be of benefit to humanity. Futhermore, a price cannot be put on knowledge, and this point may be illustrated from medicine—good health is something to be prized in its own right; the standards of the accountant are inappropriate. What is a human life worth? How does one place a value on saving one tiny baby from a premature death? This kind of goal is not to be short-circuited or held back by petty penny pinchers. It is very difficult, therefore, for administrators to control the resources of a medical school.

Similarly, there is a moral quality to campus enterprises. Irving Kristol (1972) maintains that the prototype of the intellectual is the "sermonizing cleric." In Kristol's somewhat jaundiced view, the intellectual and academic person claims the privilege of being moral guide and critic to the world. It is not, he maintains, that academics feel their arguments are right, but that they themselves are right. From the sacerdotal view, campuses should be regarded like churches—the money coming to the campus from society or from donors is almost like a tithe. Even so, just as the ultimate loyalty of the priest is to God rather than to the church, the loyalty of a scholar from this point of view is to a scholarly discipline more than to a campus.

All scholars have equal authority before the shrine of scholarship. Some may have achieved a greater degree of grace than others, but that will ultimately be decided in the light of eternal and imperishable values, a realm where the evidence is never finally in. In the meantime, it follows that, ideally, only scholars can judge other scholars. Scholars not only judge; they also hire and fire. Peer review is absolutely critical; after all, who can say who is a good chemist except another chemist?

Thus, scholars ideally should discipline one another; this ideal stems from the professional perspective. Who can really know if a surgeon has made a mistake except another surgeon? Even then, this is often a very difficult judgment, always possibly unfair. It follows that everyone's welfare is best served if professionals are given the benefit of any doubt that exists. In the absence of clear standards and objective evidence, scholars must protect one another.

From the point of view of the professional, accounting for one's work load is a problem. In a sense, professionals should not be asked to account for what they do. There are aspects of creative work that simply cannot be translated into market terms; the work has moral value. This explains a situation that often baffles administrators: Faculty members sincerely ask for a 100 percent increase in salary or for some other gigantic expenditure, even in tight financial times. From the sacerdotal point of view, the question is not what society can afford, but what the effort is worth. To return to our medical analogy, how can one count pennies when treating a burn victim? Apart from the question of whether work loads should be measured at all, professionals believe that professionals should decide how their efforts will be distributed. They believe they should decide how many courses are to be offered and what the nature of those courses is to be. Ideally, they believe, they should determine the size of the class, and they certainly should give their own accounting of their efforts. The work scholars do is not place-oriented, in the strict sense; it is not limited to the campus and cannot be exclusively judged as a campus activity. The work is best carried on where scholars work best, where colleagues of like mind exist, and where appropriate conditions for the mind as well as the body prevail. To require faculty members to be on campus for a stated period of time is, thus, inappropriate from the sacerdotal point of view.

The perspective of professionals working in sacerdotal institutions is that students are apprentices. They are colleagues in a real but junior sense. Ideally, professionals make their best contributions to student development when they train each one as though he or she were going into the academic discipline under study. The highest calling for professionals, as for some monastic orders, is to clone themselves, to train others to be keepers of the flame.

We now come to the scholar's view of administration and administrators, as derived from the sacerdotal and professional perspective. From this perspective, scholars always work with colleagues, not for bosses. The organization chart of the campus, as Harlan Cleveland (1972) points out, is conceived as a straight, horizontal line. In this view, the president of the university is the executive secretary of the colloquium. He or she is a faculty member who articulates the basic values of the faculty. When the faculty cries out for strong leadership in a president, the demand is really for one who will articulate the value systems. I remember an incident recounted to me by my father, an academic and sometime administrator. He told of a new college president greeting the faculty at the first fall gathering and saying, "I am happy to have this opportunity to meet my faculty." At that point, a senior faculty member rose and said, "Mr. President, I should enter a correction into the record. The president does not have a faculty. The faculty has a president." From this point of view, when the president speaks for the needs and interests—and in the language of—other campus constituencies, he or she is unperceiving, disloyal, or even unethical.

Below the president, other administrators are regarded as employees of the faculty. From the sacerdotal perspective, administrators are servants in the highest sense of that term. They are hired to do the work that will guarantee the integrity of the teaching, learning, and research processes. From this point of view, if the institution needs restructuring, the faculty is the body that should do it, because the faculty is perfectly capable of doing it.

It should be emphasized that the professional and sacerdotal perspectives are correct to a considerable degree. In a time when all the basic institutions of society are under fire and being questioned, campuses and professors still have high credibility with the general public. I think this indicates that, overdrawn and unrealistic as some of these perspectives might appear to an administrative group, they are not without their acceptance, and they certainly possess a significant measure of truth. The point is not to outline correct and incorrect points of view or to separate the good guys from the bad guys, but simply to delineate areas that are sources of misunderstanding between faculty and administrators, areas made the more damaging by the invisibility of their root systems.

The Secular View

As an ideal type, the secular administrative view is often radically different from the sacerdotal view. I am not the first to observe and remark that, whereas administrators, and particularly presidents, come to their positions from vastly different backgrounds, over a period of time they drift in the direction of a shared administrative perspective—a perspective that, in its turn, may not be entirely accurate, even though it has many elements of truth.

From the administrative, or secular, perspective, the university is established by society to serve society's purposes, not just to provide good jobs for the faculty. If the university fails to meet these purposes, it simply will not be supported. Society can shut down any university or cut its resources whenever it decides to do so; no bolt from the Almighty will smite even the intemperate opponents of a campus. In this view, regardless of whether the world should be organized in this way or not, the university is neither a sanctuary nor a monastery, nor are academics accountable only to one another or to some abstract standard of morality. The campus is a service institution in the highest sense of that term; nevertheless, it is established by society because it provides needed and worthwhile services.

From this point of view, of course, the faculty must be involved in the hiring of faculty colleagues, and faculty judgments, if honestly delivered, are valuable. Nevertheless, the total university in its many constituencies, represented by the administration, must also have a hand in faculty hiring. Since the university is a service institution, faculty members cannot be hired simply because colleagues are comfortable with them or feel that they would be stimulating companions. Balances must also be struck in hiring within departments as well as between departments and divisions, and adminstrators, in this view, should make such judgments. Moreover, while in an ideal world the faculty would, perhaps, have exclusive jurisdiction over the dismissal of colleagues as well as their promotion and retention, in the real world the faculty is not tough-minded enough, nor does it have a broad enough perspective on institutional needs and the attitudes of society for this task to be left exclusively within its jurisdiction, according to the secular view.

If faculty members are, indeed, the priests who serve in the cathedral, then administrators are the people who drum up support and often build the cathedral. Administrators are experts in their own right. They know how to get things done. Faculty members do not have the time, or, indeed, sometimes the interest or ability to arrange the ordinary affairs of daily campus existence and, if left to their own devices, they would not do so, according to administrators. They cannot make fundamental changes in their own organization. Kristol (1972), speaking on this subject, mentions the attempts of the University of California at Berkeley to reorganize. The author concludes, "Professors are willing to impose endless inconvenience on administrators and the general public but never on themselves" (p. 109). He defends this proposition by pointing out that studies of teaching loads never result in recommendations for increased teaching loads. From the administrative perspective, every organization must have a power hierarchy. In the university, the hierarchy is justified by the administration's specialized knowledge and skills. Furthermore, there must be rules and procedures in any organization as well as standards of performance to which people in the organization must conform. No organization can exist without such rules, formal or informal. Claims that if the rules were unwritten and informal, matters would order themselves are patently untrue, according to administrators, and there are also standards of work and effort that can be arrived at on a largely common-sense basis. Faculty members who emphasize the unquantifiable character of the creative process are usually unproductive, in the administrative view. The faculty too often confuses worrying about working with working—or so the secular administrative community believes.

Next, in this view, the public not only will intrude but has a right to intrude on the affairs of the campus, provided the intervention goes through duly established channels, that is, through administrators.

Whatever the demands of an academic discipline on a faculty member, the members of a faculty owe loyalty and service to their own campus, expressed in reasonable amounts of time spent on campus and regularly published class schedules. Such schedules are best monitored by impersonal, fair administrators who perceive the total needs of all the constituencies of the university.

Like it or not, there is a kind of a market mechanism that sustains the life of a university. If a campus were to offer only majors in Greek and no

22

students enrolled, the campus would simply close. A knowledgeable colleague, reading of the difficulties of a brilliant East Coast president supported by trustees but in continual combat with the faculty on his campus, remarked that the president ultimately was in difficulty because he imposed a market orientation for fiscal survival while completely overturning the values of the faculty, embracing survival values rather than sacerdotal values. This president is also consistent with the secular, administration tradition in insisting that questions of faculty discipline cannot be left exclusively to the faculty, since the faculty will be too protective of its own. In this view, students are seen primarily as customers rather than as apprentices, although they are, of course, other things too; if they are trainees, it is in a general sense, not in a specific, academic discipline sense. Interestingly enough, students in recent years have tended to share this orientation to a greater degree than the sacerdotal orientation of the faculty, at least as undergraduates.

Finally, administrators believe that faculty quality and output can be judged at least partly by simple observation and common sense. Administrators must play a role in this process, since professional courtesy prohibits faculty members from exercising rigorous restraints or standards over one another. From the secular point of view, the university is like any other complex multipurpose organization. It needs a chain of command and a manager, and the president is the manager. The president is there to serve the general public, that is, society, as well as the various campus constituencies. He is certainly not there as the exclusive servant of faculty interests or narrow academic values.

The managerial and secular view I have just outlined is overstated but not totally inaccurate. These broad, stereotypical pictures of two polar positions do not, of course, exhaust the subtleties of either one; nor, in all fairness, do they do justice to either one.

Misunderstanding in Action

Moving to specific instances of misunderstanding and suspicion of unethical behavior that might be explained by these two points of view, let us consider a professor who goes to Europe, carrying all of his students' grades with him. The unfulfilled computer waits panting, students fume, and administrators fulminate. From the administrative point of view, the professor is unprincipled. The professor later explains, however, that he was deeply concerned about the grades in the class and wanted more time to reflect upon them, and he asks if he is there to help the computer, or if the computer there to help him. What is a university for, if not for teaching, learning, and evaluating what has taken place? What higher obligations could a professor have? From the sacerdotal point of view, administrators are slaves to expedience; they are market-oriented, petty mechanical putterers, willing to subvert the true values of scholarship completely.

Another example of how mutual suspicion of unethical behavior is generated between the faculty and administrators is a vote expressing lack of confidence in the president of a university. The president may feel that, under his or her leadership, the university has improved in every demonstrable way: The quality of students has improved, endowments have increased, faculty members of national stature have been attracted to the campus, salaries have gone up, student applications have increased dramatically, and so on. From the president's point of view, to ignore all these gains and pass a vote of no confidence is not only childish but also positively unethical. From the faculty point of view, however, absolute values are involved, and the violation of any one is a sign of moral bankruptcy.

To return to a topic mentioned before, the question of accounting for faculty work loads is one that elicits the suspicion of unethical behavior between faculty members and administrators. Teachers are frustrated by having to explain how hard they work and what they do with their time. Because it is difficult to measure the faculty work load and impossible to do it perfectly, the faculty tends to assume that the ethical thing to do is to leave the matter to the conscience and judgment of individual faculty members; the real job of administrators is to tell off-campus investigators that it is none of their business, no matter who they are, and if that creates difficulties, then it is the administration's job to get tough. Administrators, however, believe they must respond to legitimate demands for answers to reasonable and fair questions about how faculty time is spent.

Affirmative action provides another illustration of how differing perspectives on a problem can give rise to suspicions of unethical behavior. Affirmative action presents difficulties in colleges and universities not because they are inhabited by bigots, but because the worthy person, in the mind of traditional academics, is defined as the one who is deemed so by a consensus of colleagues. There is no such thing as admission to the brotherhood by virtue of race and religion; that is supposed to be irrelevant. Affirmative action considerations, worthy as they may be from a societal point of view, represent an intrusion into the value system of the academy. This view is not shared by all academics as individuals, but it is consistent with the sacerdotal cosmology outline. The point of view opposed to this is that indifference to the rights of minorities and of women undermines basic Constitutional rights, and that campuses must subscribe to the rules laid down by the democratic society in which they exist. Therefore, outside intrusion is morally justified and demanded if affirmative action standards are not met. It is easy to see how suspicions of unethical behavior can surround such issues, even when high moral ground is taken by both sides.

From the sacerdotal point of view, when cutbacks in personnel are necessary it seems obvious that the cuts should be absorbed by letting administrators go. After all, they are there to serve the faculty, and the faculty will simply have to be satisfied with fewer services. On the other hand, the administrative perspective often dictates that the smallest possible number of administrators should be dismissed, since the basic functioning of the campus must continue, and it would make little difference if every remaining faculty member increased his or her load by a few students. Each side views the other as callous and ethically imbecile.

Similarly, when administrators insist on allocating new teachers to departments solely on the basis of enrollment, it seems to the disadvantaged academics that the standards of the countinghouse have supplanted academic considerations entirely. After all, with a few more teachers, departments with dwindling enrollment could offer a sufficiently attractive array of courses to increase the number of majors.

Here is another instance that could give rise to misunderstanding: A faculty member, feeling tired, jaded, and badly in need of an altered perspective, takes a week off in the middle of the semester to go to the Bahamas, having arranged for a colleague to take his classes. A trustee on vacation sees the teacher on the beach. The trustee is puzzled and annoyed; upon her return, she informs the president. The president, searching the records, sees no report of the absence, but finds that the classes were fully covered. From the professional and sacerdotal point of view, if colleagues are willing to put forth extra effort for what, in their judgment, is a good professional or personal reason, then that should not bother administrators. From the secular, administrative perspective, the institution is being cheated. Conversely, when the president sends a fatigued dean to a conference of marginal significance in the Bahamas, the president feels that her decision is in the best interests of both the individual and the institution and requires no further explanation. Faculty members, however, having been turned down repeatedly on travel requests, view this event as an injustice.

Calls for accountability from administrators are chronically irritating to faculty members. They persist in feeling that their activities simply cannot be meaningfully understood in statistical terms. From their point of view, the real issue is the unethical capitulation of spineless administrators to petty bureaucratic busybodies, while administrators view faculties, in their unwillingness to account for their activities and their willingess to dissemble, as unethical.

The reluctance of faculty members to discipline their own is related to the same type of professional concern that makes it difficult for physicians and attorneys to discipline one another. For example, a faculty member is accused by several students of threatening to lower their grades if they do not withdraw from the ROTC program. Administrators see this threat as a clear violation of professional ethics, but the faculty is not so certain: They would like to know more of the details and circumstances behind the professor's action, even if the accusations turn out to be correct. To take punitive action against a colleague even in a clear case of misbehavior may invite administrative outsiders to intervene in cases that are less clear. The coolness of many faculty members to the establishment of a student grade-appeal process is understandable in view of their assumptions, but this moral indifference to due process strikes administrators as questionable.

Perhaps the president pressures the dean to admit a student who is marginally qualified to an overcrowded program. The department chairman resists the president on grounds that are obvious. The president, in this instance, decides not to overrule the department and offers a somewhat lame explanation to the politician who was pressuring him. He discovers that the mother of the student has been to see the dean personally, and that the dean has already admitted the student. The ethical suspicions on both sides of this incident should not be surprising.

Again, a member of the psychology department who has a private psychotherapy practice in off hours places the university phone number on his business card and uses it freely. From his perspective as a professional, his outside consulting work for extra remuneration is really a part of his overall responsibilities. The cost of the phone service to the university is negligible and fully justified, from his perspective. From the administrative view, however, the use of university facilities for private profit to any degree and in any form is unacceptable. Nevertheless, the administration has raised no question about some blurring of the lines where the medical faculty is concerned. Thus we see that there are differences in circumstances and perspectives that predispose administrators and faculties to accuse each other of unethical behavior. Again, we are dealing, in most instances, not so much with ethics as we are with perceptual issues. Administrators tend to be viewed as Machiavellian, shortsighted, market-oriented, high-handed individuals who are too susceptible to parochial pressures from outside the campus. Administrators, in turn, have built-in biases that lead them to see faculty as impractical, self-indulgent, self-serving, careless of standards and procedures when it serves their purpose to be so, and in other ways on the verge of ethical dereliction. The problem is further complicated when faculty members or administrators seem to embrace the values and perspectives of the other, to the confusion of everyone. For example, a faculty member holds two fully-paid positions in two different universities a hundred miles apart. The faculty member defends herself by saying she is interested only in output. She has unusual energy and is able to perform in ways that totally satisfy her obligation to both institutions. Now it is the administrator's turn to squirm. The two argue: "But scholarship involves more than just classes meeting and keeping office hours and serving on a minor committee or two. There is a need for reflection, research, and even meditation about the problems of the field—processes that are disrupted by too heavy a work schedule." "All right," the faculty member replies, "Then what's all this nonsense about accountability and upping the work load, with which the administration has been assaulting the faculty for so long?"

The confusion arises because the faculty member has, in a sense, accepted the secular, administrative view, but is presenting it as a burlesque.

Administrators, however, are prone to the view that many faculty members have already sacrificed their sacerdotal and scholarly values and are really interested in the values of the market themselves. They complain that they are dealing with people who claim to care nothing about money but who all want what money can buy.

The Role of the President

If this is a useful analysis, then where does it leave the president, other than in the uncomfortable middle? What is the role of the president? To supply secular perspective to the sacerdotal faculty? To explain the sacerdotal view to uncomprehending administrative colleagues, legislators, donors, and the general public? Will explanation do any good? Won't most off-campus constituencies simply dismiss the sacerdotal, professional view as irrelevant? Finally, if—as seems obvious—the role of the president is to mediate between these two worlds of perception, are there any techniques presidents can apply to fulfill that role?

It is critical for presidents to understand that these two perspectives exist on campus for a number of reasons. In ways we do not totally understand, the president plays a fundamental part in setting the attitudinal tone of a campus. His or her influence is not exclusive, of course; others, both on the faculty and in the administration, are also influential. In moments of crisis and transition, however—and, perhaps, more than presidents are aware—the president fixes the mood and spirit of interchange. If a president accepts the view that professionals see themselves in different ways, and that this view helps establish a harmonious climate, and if the president also understands that administrators' views are just as necessary as the sacerdotal perspective, then this conviction is communicated in a hundred ways to others. It is this healing view that helps hold things together and allows campuses to function in creative ways. Resentments are pandemic in academic communities, and, perhaps, in all stressed organizations in transition. Resentments arise not so often from the actions of others as from interpretations of those actions.

The president's task as ethical leader is not to try to achieve academic sainthood; it is his or her task to provide healing interpretations to the academic community. We are dealing, for the most part, with sincere and dedicated people who quite genuinely share different perspectives on ethical behavior. It is the president's job to mediate and arrive at creative solutions. Some tension is inevitable, since virtue resides in both the sacerdotal and the secular point of view. It is the job of the president to create an environment where dialectical change is encouraged, where people deal with one another not as scoundrels but as colleagues, and where different interests and perspectives may be compromised in ways that resolve tension and permit action.

Since the two worlds I have described do not simply proceed on their own tracks but are constantly in collision with one another, the role of the president is not simply to be an interpreter; the devices and artifices of leadership must continually be called into play. Sometimes the president must set the limits of acceptable and unacceptable behavior and clearly explain the reasons for his or her position. Sometimes this requires the president to explain the professional role of academics to the uncomprehending general public. Society does dimly recognize that professionals require freedom and latitude if they are to function effectively and serve society well. More frequently, perhaps, the president will need to interpret the legitimate demands of the secular view to academic professionals. Here, too, although levels of awareness will vary, academics also recognize that their world is perceived differently by outsiders. A president will seldom be dealing with ideologues or zealots.

As for the techniques by which a president may address his or her formidable task, I leave that discussion to the genius and skill of my colleagues who preside over dynamic campuses in these difficult but exciting times. The president's job is formidable, but on balance, and most of the time, it is rewarding. The president's job is to bring heaven and earth together without creating a hell for either the faculty or administrators.

References

Cleveland, H. *The Future Executive.* New York: Harper & Row, 1972.
Etzioni, A. *Modern Organizations.* Englewood Cliffs, N.J.: Prentice-Hall, 1964.
Kristol, I. *On the Democratic Idea in America.* New York: Harper & Row, 1972.

Donald E. Walker is president of Southeasterr
Massachusetts University. He is the author
of a number of publications in the areas
of counseling, collective bargaining, and the
role of the college and university president.
His most recent book is The Effective Administrator
(San Francisco: Jossey-Bass, 1979).

Sexual harassment: What is it? Who does it? Who are its victims? What are its consequences? Can or should anything be done about it?

Sexual Harassment of Women Students

Susan Margaret Vance

In the spring of 1978, the National Advisory Council on Women's Educational Programs, a body appointed by the President to report on enforcement of Title IX of the 1972 Educational Amendments to the 1964 Civil Rights Act,* decided to address questions about sexual harassment from the point of view of students who have experienced sexual harassment on campus. As a first step, the Council commissioned a legal analysis of the problem, as such analysis had developed in the courts, to determine whether sexual harassment in nonemployment, educational contexts was properly considered an actionable federal issue. That analysis, published in the summer of 1978, indicated that certain kinds of sexual harassment involving students could be dealt with under Title IX as prohibited, sex-based discrimination.

The Council subsequently developed a call for information to determine the nature and the extent of the problem on campuses in this country. This call was sent to student governments, deans of students, and professional organizations, in the hope that it would reach those who had

*Copies of the National Advisory Council report are available from: National Advisory Council on Women's Educational Programs, 1832 M Street, N. W., Suite 821, Washington, D.C. 20036.

directly encountered the problem. The process was very slow, and personal contact was clearly a significant factor in obtaining responses. The responses came primarily from postsecondary educational institutions, both private and public, with only a few responses from elementary or secondary institutions. The call requested the respondent to state the type of harassment, the setting in which the incident took place, whether the incident was reported, and the eventual outcome.

The Council reached the following conclusions: There is a problem; it can be defined sufficiently to be addressed; sexual harassment is done innocently by many, and consciously by few; the victims of sexual harassment have little in common other than their gender; serious offenders can be identified; perpetrators are usually "repeaters," and there appear to be definite patterns among heavy offenders; the victims often drop out of school, change majors or careers, and otherwise imagine that they can cope with the problem alone; no legal solution can be found without help from the campuses.

The responses that are the basis of the Council's forthcoming report range from accounts of ill-placed repartee to outright rape. None of these incidents is trivial, and many of them would not have happened if the educational institutions involved had enforced firm, well-publicized prohibitions against sexual harassment and had easily accessible procedures for handling complaints.

The Council's report is set out in two parts. The first section is a general analysis of the problem and its ramifications—for example, the meaning of the term, its causes, its victims, its perpetrators, its consequences, and the way educational institutions are attempting to address it. The second section is technical and sets forth the methodology of the report, statistical results of the study, the legal theory of sexual harassment as prohibited discrimination, and the management of institutional liability. The summary of the findings and the Council's recommendation will be included in an executive overview accompanying the report.

There is a climate in this country that is now allowing issues like sexual harassment to emerge. Relief under circumstances where there have been proved instances of harassment, and where academic institutions have been convinced of the existence of a problem with respect to a particular individual, can take many creative forms. Termination of federal funds or firing the aggressor is not the only solution and is often not appropriate to address the problem. Other solutions such as suspending a professor without pay for a quarter have served as adequate warning to persons committing substantial offenses. At some point on the continuum, there is an appropriate solution to each problem.

What then, in this framework, constitutes sexual harassment? It is more than a wink, yet less then a seduction. As a recent character in a television program on sexual harassment asked, "Are you telling me 'horsing around' constitutes an actionable offense?'' The answer, cautiously, is yes.

If we reflect on the past, we may remember incidents that passed without notice or understanding at the time they occurred. One of my roommates in college experienced sexual harassment with her senior faculty advisor, who was in charge of her honors program. One afternoon when she went to see him to discuss her paper, he locked the door, put the key in his pocket, and chased her around the office. Only when she banged on the door loudly enough to cause the secretary to bang on the door from the opposite side did he consent to open the door and allow her to leave. Three days later she was finally able to talk to someone about the incident. She subsequently refused to let us do anything about it because she was concerned that she would be prevented from completing her honors paper or would receive too low a grade to graduate.

Sexual harassment is a topic that has been raised repeatedly by people who are seeking to understand what it is and what it is not, and who, for the most part, question whether women really experience encounters of this kind. I have found myself searching for a way to convey what men simply have no reference for and do not understand. A recent book by Esme Dodderidge, *The New Gulliver or The Adventures of Lemuel Gulliver, Jr., in Capovolta,* presents the problem in terms that men may be able to comprehend.

In the course of a business trip, a modern-day Gulliver finds himself in a foreign land where the roles of men and women are reversed—the land of Capovolta. After an awkward period of adjustment, he begins to look for work, and he finds himself addressing a team of four women, urging them to let him use his skills as a space technologist instead of wasting himself on mere household chores. The exchange between Gulliver, called Klemo in Capovolta, and his superior, Avgard, focuses our specific concerns:

> She smiled at me very kindly and approvingly.
>
> "Klemo, my dear boy, I'm really very proud of you, and very pleased with you. It was splendid the way you fired up like that and put those three silly creatures out of countenance. It was admirable."
>
> "Thank you, Avgard. It is kind of you to say so. I'm afraid I was rather rude and must have sounded insufferably conceited, but there seemed to be no other way of getting you all to take me seriously."
>
> "Ah, Klemo, dear lad, I take you very seriously." And with that she moved up against me so unexpectedly and so rapidly for a woman of her bulk, that I found myself trapped between her and the choir-stall arrangement where my interlocutors had been sitting. "You look very handsome, you know, when you are angry. You are so delightfully masculine. I find you rather an exciting person."

"Avgard, no!" I exclaimed, pushing her hand away in real horror. It seemed not only undignified but almost disgusting to me that this elderly, respected woman should behave in this wanton way.

I could not help recalling a story told to me by my wife . . . about an old professor whose interest in the young women studying under his guidance was centered in other portions of their persons than the minds he was supposed to be training. . . . I could not altogether prevent some sneaking sympathy with this old man at the time. . . . [T]he resentment that she and her friends felt at his refusal to recognize their rights as individual persons to bestow or withhold favors where they chose. . . [N]ow I had a great deal more sympathy for and understanding of their point of view.

Dodderidge's portrayal of Klemo's dilemma helps articulate a problem that might otherwise seem elusive, but sexual harassment is not always so graphic. Indeed, the range of behavior that can be called sexual harassment is so great that there is considerable confusion about the meaning of the phrase, even for those who acknowledge that the problem exists. Rather than choose among the myriad and often conflicting definitions of sexual harassment currently in use, the Council decided to issue its call without a definition, in hopes of obtaining a clearer picture of the problem from the responses themselves. (A number of working definitions appear at the end of this chapter.)

Significantly, the reports revealed that the definition results from the effect rather than the intent of the action; in many cases, the perpetrator does not appear to understand his behavior as harassment of any kind. Offensive touching is not something that is an actionable offense in and of itself unless it is repeated and becomes a perpetual problem between a particular student and a particular professor. When the problem is persistent despite repeated objections, the institution should attempt to help the offender in question break the habit. Some methods of persuasion are more helpful than others. Men serving in positions of power—chairmen of departments, chairmen of committees, guidance counselors—appear to be much more frequently accused of sexual harassment than do men whose primary interaction with students is in the classroom. Offenders include older men, men who focus their offensive actions on younger women, and on those younger, newly arrived faculty members who seem to have difficulty making the distinction between themselves as recent gradute students and newly arrived teachers. A previously unobjectionable relationship that has changed but in which a man continues to attempt to impose his will can result in sexual harassment.

Respondents described wider ranges of incidents as sexual harassment than present definitions permit. The spectrum included rapes as well as nonsalacious slurs on women. Respondents often distinguished between offers to reward sexual cooperativeness and promises to punish resistance. The two were not always associated with each other, and interchanges did not routinely escalate from requests to demands. Sexual overtures devoid of any promise or threat were described by a number of women as sexual harassment, especially when repeated. Each individual student established her own threshold of tolerance of sexual harassment, but only sexual demands backed up by threats were consistently described as instances of sexual harassment.

The responses received by the Council have been easily categorized into five classifications: (1) nonsalacious, gender-charged slurs, suggestive or salacious remarks or actions, referred to more simply as general sexual remarks and behavior; (2) inappropriate, sanction-free sexual advances, or, more simply, "come-ons"; (3) solicitation of sexual activity by promises of reward—the "come-on" with a promise; (4) coercion of sexual activity by threat of punishment—the "come-on" with punishment; and (5) sexual crimes and misdemeanors.

While these categories do not always occur exclusively separate and apart from each other, they do conform to the rough hierarchy of the incidents that were reported. In any case, two elements are apparent in the responses and have provided a basis for the definition of sexual harassment in the Council's report. First, there is gender alignment in formal, sexually neutral relationships (for example, teacher-student, counselor-patient). All forms of sexual harassment involve emphasis on the gender of the person harassed, either sexually or in more encompassing sociobiological terms. Second, the person who is subjected to sexual harassment finds the gender alignment objectionable. In this context, the motive or the intent of the initiator is secondary, and the disposition of the person who is the object of harassment is the primary determining factor.

Obviously, not all forms of unwanted gender alignment in human relations are illegal, but viable legal theory is emerging to support allegations of sexual harassment in the area of employment law. In April 1980, the United States Equal Employment Opportunity Commission (EEOC), which administers Title VII of the 1964 Civil Rights Act, issued interim guidelines containing a definition of illegal sexual harassment:

> Harassment on the basis of sex is a violation of Section 703 of Title VII. Unwelcomed sexual advances, request for sexual favors, and other verbal or physical conduct of a sexual nature, constitutes sexual harassment when (1) submission to such conduct is made either explicitly or implicitly a term or condition of an individual's employment; (2) submission to or rejection of such conduct by an individual is used as a basis for employment decisions affecting such individuals; (3) such conduct has the purpose or effect of substan-

tially interfering with the individual's work performance or creating or intimidating hostile or an offensive work environment (U.S. Equal Employment Opportunity Commission, 1980).

The EEOC guidelines and the emerging line of cases in employment discrimination demonstrate that sexual harassment in employment has been considered discrimination on the basis of sex and has the following characteristics: (1) It is objectionable action unwelcome to its recipient; (2) the content of the act involves a demand for sexual activity or conduct of a sexual nature; (3) it is visited upon one or more, but not necessarily all, members of only one gender by the initiator; (4) it is constituted by either the intention of the initiator or the effect of the action; (5) initiators may be any persons in positions to affect substantially the working environment or terms and conditions of the recipient's employment; and (6) the employer is liable when acquiescence is demonstrated by failure to protect the victim.

The primary federal statute prohibiting sex discrimination against students is Title IX. While Title IX does not explicitly prohibit sexual harassment, the only litigation related to this question indicates that coverage is highly likely. The analogy of sexual harassment in employment to an educational context can be made by rewording the EEOC characteristics in the following way: It is objectionable to the recipient; it is visited upon one or more members of only one gender by the initiator; the intent or effect of the act is deleterious to the recipient; and the institution cannot show that it has protected the recipient.

When does an educational institution become liable for the sexual harassment of a student? This liability may accrue from direct or indirect contractual obligations, under tort law, by statute, by regulatory provisions or rules, or by provisions of a state or of the United States Constitution. The source of the liability determines the forum in which the matter will be addressed.

Successful employers have been those who encourage people with problems to come forward and talk about them. To pay attention to the person raising the issue is crucial. Finding liability at the institutional or court level is not the only satisfactory solution; it is important, however, not to back away from the problem, but to face it and deal with it. For some time, I have been concerned about the unwillingness or reticence in academic communities to deal with these questions. Confidentiality is a concern, and so are unfounded accusations. When problems are as idiosyncratic as these, each one must be dealt with on its own merits, and a highly visible procedure for resolving the problem may be a very helpful deterrent. There are many ways to approach the question of sexual harassment; placing women in positions of authority to deal with complaints is one solution.

A line of cases is beginning to emerge that articulates the limits of employer liability for the sexual harassment of employees by other employees; as yet, however, no direct applications have emerged in federal common law in which students are the focal point. Arguably, an educational institution has a responsibility toward its students equal to that of an employer toward employees, particularly where that duty is defined by two federal civil rights statutes as similar as Title VII and Title IX. Title VII cases and agency interpretations of this issue are therefore instructive in the context of Title IX, except perhaps where Title IX places a greater or explicitly different type of obligation on educational institutions with respect to students.

Most of the Title VII employment litigation on the issue of sexual harassment has turned on one or more of three elements—proof, notice, and consequence. A look at the potential extrapolation of complaints under Title VII is appropriate. First, plaintiffs are required to convince the court that the incident occurred as alleged. This burden is traditionally high, particularly in this area, where it is not uncommon to meet the assumption that accusations are easy to make and difficult to prove. The analogy at this point to criminal prosecution of rape cases is only too obvious. Demonstrating a pattern by showing that similar offenses of sexual harassment have been committed with other victims does not prove that the disputed incident occurred, but it may buttress the original charge. In addition, plaintiffs have been required to show that the consequences of sexual harassment were harmful to them, and that they gave notice of the harassment to their employers. One of the leading Title VII cases on this issue is *Miller* v. *Bank of America* (1979), in which it was held that a plaintiff was not required to give formal notice to the employer or to use the available internal grievance procedures prior to filing a lawsuit. Several lower federal district courts, however, have ruled that a precondition for a valid Title VII charge is ratification of the sexual harassment by the employer. This can be shown by evidence that the employer had actual or constructive knowledge of the incident and acquiesced in it by failing to do anything about the problem

While a complaint or other formal notice to an employer is not the sole criterion by which knowledge may be imputed, the area in dispute between the Ninth Circuit in *Miller* and the lower district court opinion in that case appears to revolve around this aspect of notice. Most district court decisions have required the plaintiff to show an adverse relationship between the sexual harassment and the plaintiff's terms or conditions of employment. The EEOC guidelines support this requirement, but construe it liberally to include as actionable the creation or acceptance of an intimidating, hostile, or offensive working environment.

What, then, are the implications of the Title VII employment law for Title IX? Title IX in education has greater statutory breadth with respect to this issue than Title VII has in its respective jurisdiction of employment. This is primarily because the language of Title IX prohibits discrimination regardless of the source, while Title VII prohibits discrimination only by employers. One potential implication of this greater breadth in Title IX might be a lower threshold of consequence necessary to establish an actionable claim and, therefore, diminished requirements for notice.

The published Title IX regulations require all institutions within the jurisdiction of the regulation to adopt and publish grievance procedures providing for prompt and equitable resolutions of student complaints alleging any action that would be prohibited by Title IX. Because the responsibility of educational institutions to students under Title IX encompasses broader and more varied contexts than responsibilities imposed by other federal statutes, both public and private educational institutions should develop grievance procedures, particularly with respect to questions of sexual harassment addressed today. Several creative grievance procedures have been developed, and these have been set forth in the report of the Council.

If sexual harassment is a prohibited form of sex discrimination under Title IX—and the evidence suggests that it is—it follows that the mandatory grievance procedures must be capable of providing prompt and equitable resolution of sexual harassment complaints brought by students. Grievance procedures without this capability would not satisfy the requirement of the regulation and may in and of themselves constitute noncompliance with federal regulations. For a complaint under Title IX to be viable, then, one consequence of this regulatory requirement of a grievance procedure is likely to be a requirement for the plaintiff to show that the educational institution's grievance procedure is incapable of providing prompt and equitable relief.

What is required in terms of proof is not clear in the case law yet. Proof of other instances, or allegations of other, corroborating instances, are helpful and would tend to persuade a court. A viable grievance procedure clearly exists when an educational institution provides a place or a person to address these concerns, when the institution is consistently receptive to the problems that are presented, and when attempts are made to address these issues. Institutional liability is more likely to be avoided if the institution is clearly receptive to concerns and if an attempt is made without delay to address the problem somehow.

A myth has been perpetuated in this society about educational institutions. Just as people look to lawyers for solutions to problems, so do people believe educational institutions do not make mistakes, and that they have an operational system of checks and balances that assures that decisions will be fair and equitable. There was a time when courts steadfastly held to a "hands-off" or minimal scrutiny policy, based on the assumption that only the educational institutions could adequately and correctly address the problems they confronted. That certainly was true in *Johnson v. University of Pittsburgh* (1977); the courts determined that they had insufficient understanding of the problems to be able to judge or evaluate the decisions that administrators at educational institutions make, but those days are gone.

With cases like *Sweeney* v. *The Board of Trustees of Keene State College* (1979) and *Kunda* v. *Muhlenberg College* (1980), the courts have begun to treat educational institutions like other institutions and to hold these institutions accountable for their action or inaction, their decision or nondecision. In light of *Cannon* v. *The University of Chicago, et al.* (1979), it is clear that when a problem of sexual harassment is not resolved on campus, there is a legal forum that will entertain students' complaints, whether the campus agencies created to address the problem do or not.

This country has long been dedicated to the concept of providing an environment conducive to learning. When respect is absent in relationships between students and their faculty and administrators, learning is impeded, and the academic community essential to this process begins to disintegrate. The problem of disrespect must be addressed; only then, in an environment free of invidious distractions, can each person participate in an unrestrained academic interchange.

What is at stake is often not simply a grade or a recommendation for a student, but also access to a discipline or an entire career. Administrators still have an opportunity to address this problem without relying on institutions such as courts to make judgments. But if they fail to address the problem, the courts will.

We need to ensure that women will have equal access to the same learning experience we provide men—an environment free of the kind of invidious negative behavior that detracts from the learning process, that undermines the primary function of the classroom, and that prevents the learning experience from taking place. One response the Council received illustrates the invidious behavior in question:

> This semester one of my graduate professors started the first class session asking the women in the class if they would like recreational sex. The second question session went the same way. In the third session, after he found out which women were married, he asked me why I wasn't married. During the fourth session, he asked me what I thought love was. I was trying not to apply the term to myself in the sexual manner, even though I felt that was what he wanted me to say. Then he said "Well, what would you do if I said I loved you?" I said that I would say no, but because it was my choice to remain independent, not because I disliked him as a person. He then said "Well, what would you say if I said that I wanted to make

love to you?" Again, I said no. Then, after he made a reference to how a larger man could just overpower a smaller woman, he gave an example of how he could just go ahead and do anything he wanted. He then said if he could do anything, he could just go ahead and rape me. When I asked him what he would do when he was brought in to be tried, he said that he would just lie. When he adjourned the class that night, he told everybody that they could all go except me. I did stay after and asked him what he wanted. He just started complimenting me on what a fine lawyer he thought I would be. As we left the classroom, he started toward his office while trying to continue his conversaton with me. I turned in the other direction and said goodbye. By this time, I felt quite sure that he might have done something if I had let the situation continue.

Sexual harassment is not an experience that men and women share. Why is this behavior tolerated, when it is clearly unwanted and counter-productive in the learning environment? Sexual harassment, whether real or perceived, is a problem that will not subside. It is not a problem people can sit and discuss, hoping that eventually the right answer will emerge; we must address it, sooner rather than later. Sexual harassment is an issue of the 1980s, in all spheres and at all levels of our society. The myths that have protected educational institutions from intrusion by the courts are disappearing, and institutions will be expected to deal with sexual harassment on the campuses, just as IBM and the Bank of America have been forced to do.

Definitions of Sexual Harassment

". . .[S]exual harassment in the classroom . . . [is] harassment in which the faculty member covertly or overtly uses the power inherent in the status of a professor to threaten, coerce or intimidate a student to accept sexual advances or risk reprisal in terms of a grade, a recommendation, or even a job."
Assistant Vice-President Shirley Clark, University of Minnesota, quoted by Anne Truax. "Application of Feminism: The Resolution of Sexual Harassment Cases," April 1979.

". . . [S]exual harassment is broader than sexual coercion . . . [and] can only be understood as the confluence of authority relations *and* sexual interest in a society stratified by gender."
Thesis by Donna Benson. University of California, 1979.

"Sexual harassment is not a sexual issue, it is an issue of power."
Thesis by Judy Oshinsky. University of Miami, Florida, 1979.

"Sexual harassment . . . refers to the unwanted imposition of sexual requirements in the context of a relationship of unequal power. Central to the concept is the use of power derived from one social sphere to lever benefits or impose deprivations in another. . . . When one is sexual, the other material, the cumulative sanction is particularly potent.

"Sexual harassment may occur as a single encounter or as a series of incidents at work. I may place a sexual condition upon employment opportunities at a clearly defined threshold . . . or it may occur as a pervasive or continuing condition of the work environment. Extending along the continuum of severity, . . . examples include verbal suggestions or jokes, constant leering or ogling, brushing against your body 'accidentally,' a friendly pat, squeeze or pinch or arm against you, catching you alone for a quick kiss, the indecent proposition backed by the threat of losing your job, and forced sexual relations. Complex forms include the persistent innuendo and the continuing threat which is never consummated either sexually or economically. The most straightforward example is 'put out or get out.'"

> Catharine A. MacKinnon. *Sexual Harassment of Working Women.* New Haven, Conn.: Yale University Press, 1979.

"Sexual harassment is . . . unsolicited nonreciprocal male behavior that asserts a woman's sex role over her function as a worker. . . .

"It can be any of all of the following: staring at, commenting upon, or touching a woman's body; requests for acquiescence in sexual behavior; repeated nonreciprocated propositions for dates, demands for sexual intercourse; and rape. . . . Sexual harassment is . . . an act of aggression at any stage of its expressions, and in all its forms it contributes to the ultimate goal of keeping women subordinate at work."

> Lin Farley. *Sexual Shakedown: Sexual Harassment of Women on the Job,* McGraw-Hill, 1978.

"Sexual harassment . . . imposes a requirement of sexual cooperation as a condition of . . . advancement."

> Memorandum to Faculty and Staff of Rutgers University from President Bloustein, 1979.

"Any unwanted sexual leers, suggestions, comments, or physical contact which you find objectionable."

> Working Women's Institute, New York, 1978.

"Whereas in rape cases, the man overpowers a woman with a weapon or threat of loss of life, in sexual harassment he overtly or implicitly threatens her with loss of livelihood, or with academic failure and hence loss of future livelihood."

> Project on the Status and Education of Women, Association of American Colleges, Washington, D.C., 1978.

40

"Definitions of sexual harassment vary depending on the sex, employment, or ideology of the definer. Most feminists are willing to accept a broad definition, which places degrees of harassment along a continuum ranging from sexist remarks to rape."

Anne Truax, director, Women's Center,
University of Minnesota, 1979.

References

Cannon v. *University of Chicago, et al.,* 99 S. Ct. 1946, 441 U.S. 667 (1979).
Dodderidge, E. *The New Gulliver or The Adventures of Lemuel Gulliver, Jr., in Capovolta.* New York: Taplinger, 1979.
Johnson v. *University of Pittsburgh,* 435 Fed. Supp. 1328 (2d Circuit, 1977).
Kunda v. *Muhlenberg College,* 463 F. Supp. 294, 22 FEP 62, (3rd Circuit, 1980).
Miller v. *Bank of America,* 600 F 2d 211, 20 FEP Cases 462 (9th Circuit, 1979).
Sweeney v. *Board of Trustees,* 20 FEP 759 (1st, 1979).

Susan Vance serves as chair of the Presidentially appointed National Advisory Council on Women's Educational Programs. A practicing attorney holding a J.D. degree from DePaul College of Law in Chicago, Ms. Vance specializes in labor law, Civil Rights Law, and family law. She is the chairperson of the Illinois State Bar Association's Long-Range Planning Committee and has published articles on the subjects of labor law and sex discrimination in schools.

Examines abuses and unethical practices in the recruitment of students.

Ethical Issues in Recruiting Students

Edward B. Fiske

Not long ago, a northern Kentucky university decided that to attract more students it would budget about $25,000 for scholarships. The staff printed scholarship vouchers and put them inside some of several hundred balloons. Officials planned to go to a park in downtown Cincinnati, which is one of the drawing areas for the university, and set them aloft. Anybody who could manage to retrieve one of the balloons containing a voucher could show up at the university and receive a scholarship.

UPI sent out some wire copy about the idea. (As a matter of fact, the university still receives letters from people around the world who want to study in an American university, because the story was circulated on the international UPI wire.) The people in the state education department heard about the scheme and suggested to the university that this was not the most dignified way of recruiting students. The clincher came, though, when students in the area began arming themselves with bows and arrows and BB guns to shoot the balloons down. Some clearer heads decided that this particular promotional scheme might be a threat to public safety, and on the eve of the balloon launching, it was cancelled.

The experience of this college was something of a parable for higher education in general. I certainly do not have to spend any time explaining the reasons why ethical considerations regarding recruitment are becoming more important or are at least getting more attention in higher education these days. Obviously, the demographic changes are the key ones—the decline in the numbers of college-age youth, and the shift for colleges from a seller's to a buyer's market. The fact that, for many colleges, it is increasingly the student rather than the college making the choice is reinforced by inflation: Increasing costs are tempting some colleges, at least some that are relatively less attractive than others, to engage in behavior that is at best questionable.

Benefits of Tight Times

Before discussing the problems of recruitment itself, I want to emphasize that there are some positive effects of the situation in which colleges now find themselves. Colleges are having to rethink their reasons for being. They can no longer assume, either in their catalogues or in general terms, that college education is a good thing in its own right or that there is a clearcut value to a liberal-arts education. The demographic shift has precipitated a healthy reexamination of the purpose inherent in colleges and universities. It has forced them to look both at themselves and to the needs of students, and we should not lose sight of the benefits and the importance of this self-examination.

Second, colleges are restructuring their curriculums, and this is also all for the good. Although much attention has been directed toward the new Harvard "core curriculum" program, most colleges with serious liberal-arts faculties are engaged in this process.

Third, colleges are also becoming more businesslike and efficient in their administration. This, too, is positive. In the 1950s and the early 1960s, it was said to be impossible to mismanage an American university, since it was easy to cover mistakes with new programs or with additional money from somewhere. This is no longer possible. Nowhere is this change more conspicuous than in marketing. For instance, in a fascinating piece in the *Chronicle of Higher Education* some time ago, Richard Moll, formerly admissions director at Bowdoin and Vassar and now at the University of California at Santa Cruz, told about going to Bowdoin and discovering that the cover of the college prospectus featured a picture of a very morose man with a book. Moll changed that to "lobster pots, sunsets, and the Maine coast." Many marketing consultants are willing to help colleges target certain kinds of students and develop promotional brochures and other procedures by which to tap this target clientele. At their best, these consultants are aiding the positive process of colleges rethinking their missions, goals, objectives, and strategies.

Nonprofit colleges, as they involve themselves in marketing, are doing what the proprietary schools have been doing all along—they are becoming both more efficient and more flexible in meeting the consumer demands. Some time ago, the *New York Times* reported on Wellford Wilms's study at the University of California at Los Angeles, of what is effective vocational education. Wilms found, among other things, that the proprietary schools in his sample were more successful in securing jobs for their graduates than the community colleges, because the proprietary institutions were more flexible and market-oriented. Thus, there seem to be at least some positive results from the trend toward greater sensitivity to the student market. Colleges that have indulged in fuzzy rhetoric and simply assumed they were doing noble things are now being forced to rethink exactly what they are doing and to examine themselves with respect to the needs of students. This, of course, is the essence of marketing.

Abuses in Recruitment

While this institutional improvement is occurring, there is an enormous potential for abuse, and some colleges are leaping into the vacuum and committing these abuses.

Gimmickry. I am fascinated by the imaginative gimmickry to which some institutions resort in order to market their products. There was, for instance, a college that handed out monogramed Frisbees on the beaches at Ford Lauderdale to bring its name to the attention of potential students. Another college raffled off bicycles at a state fair to get names and addresses for a mailing list. Still another institution sent out a letter that began, "Congratulations! You've been accepted. . . ." Clearly, it was not a selective school. The Rochester Institute of Technology came up with one of the more ingenious ideas: On its 150th anniversary, it awarded 150 postnatal scholarships designated for children born during the time of its anniversary celebration.

Deception. Ethical considerations are especially relevant to truth in advertising. Some colleges, for example, stoop to outright lying. In my files, I have one college catalogue that pictures a boy and a girl strolling by a waterfall; in truth, there is no waterfall within 400 miles of the school. Theodore Marchasi of Barat College in Chicago, who has been involved in the truth-in-catalogue movement, says that some colleges have crossed the line from promoting education as a route to the good life to selling themselves as the good life itself, where "everything is couples holding hands under trees." Their ads are replete with water images and blatant sexuality, conveying the invitation "Come to us and be beautiful and successful." Perhaps the ultimate in this approach was a prospectus cover showing students sitting in little clusters around the usual small lake. A close look at one group showed that they were passing around a marijuana joint. I do not know whether the administration was aware of or understood the picture, nor do I really want to know, but it certainly was an amusing opening to the prospectus.

Payment for Enrollees. Other areas of abuse in recruiting students include the payment of staff or representatives on the basis of the students they recruit. The National Association of College Admissions Counselors' code of professional conduct includes a ban on the use of such headhunters. It is very clear to me, having talked to some college officials who formerly used headhunters, that the NACAC code has had some effect, preventing a number of colleges from using such practices and making admissions directors more conscious of their professionalism and more willing to stay within the professional code.

No-Need Scholarships. Another area that raises ethical issues of recruiting is "no-need" scholarships. The battle to make scholarships dependent on financial need as opposed to a simple reward for academic achievement was a hard-fought one and was won by the mid- to late 1950s. Because it addressed the problem of assuring maximum access to higher education, it was an important victory. Now, however, many colleges are beginning to offer scholarships if a student's admissions score is merely at a certain level, with the amount of aid determined by a formula. The process is one of buying good students. Colleges realize that if they are going to compete in a declining market, they need to have a reputation for quality. The *sine qua non* of survival in the 1980s is to have quality at least in certain areas. Colleges see no-need scholarships as a way of boosting the academic level of the student body. While this may make sense in the short run, in the long run all it does is raise costs for everybody throughout the whole system.

Early Deadlines. Another ethical problem is early deadlines for admission or housing. I have recently begun to hear many complaints, especially from the private sector, about the public sector using early deadlines as a way of committing students to particular institutions. Most highly selective colleges hold to April 15 as the date when they send out acceptance notices, with replies due from students by May 1. Many students, however, are finding that when they apply to a state university, it may ask them to reply by February. An applicant may respond, "But I'm really not going to know about these other schools until a little later." The school replies, "Then we cannot guarantee you housing. To guarantee housing, we want a $500 deposit by March 1." The problem is further complicated because financial aid decisions are often not made until as late as July. Thus, if a school that the student hopes to attend is dependent on a grant, the student is torn. There must be more ethical scrutiny on this question of whether we are exploiting students when we use pressure tactics to influence those who may be wavering for one reason or another about coming to our institutions.

Overadmission. Some schools that are often filled up in a high-demand program know from experience that there will be a certain amount of attrition during the first semester, and so they admit more students than they can enroll and then say, "We can't take you now, but we'll take you in January. In the meantime, you can go anywhere you want, and we'll recognize your credits." The student then enters a local community college, which, acting in good faith, plans for the student to be around during the whole year. But then January comes, and there are some spaces at the first college—off goes the student. This is a disingenuous policy. It is not widespread but it occurs often enough for complaints about it to arise.

Abuse in Recruiting Foreign Students

The most obvious abuses involve foreign students, and this is a subject about which much has been written recently. Obviously, a significant number of colleges see enrolling foreign students as an effective way to fill seats left empty because of the declining birth rate. Unfortunately, the information available to students in other countries about American colleges is inadequate. Except in places like Mexico City and other large capitals that have information centers and libraries with trained staffs, it is difficult for foreign students to get good information about American colleges and universities. I was talking to one recruiter, a headhunter, who told me that he was in the library of a U.S. information center when a boy came in wanting information about going to dental school in the United States. The officer in charge directed him to a row of catalogues on the shelf and said, "Look under the D's." Between Denison and the University of Denver there was nothing that said "dentist," and so the boy shrugged his shoulders and left.

There is also very little coordination of information from this country. A few colleges become known abroad, sometimes because they have a tradition of recruiting in certain foreign countries. Indiana for example, has been involved in South America for half a century. There is really no systematic way in which such institutions can redirect surplus applicants to other schools that might have openings.

Then, of course, there is the problem of the headhunters. You will recall the story of Windham College in Vermont, which closed a couple of years ago and left scores of foreign students stranded. They had been recruited by a headhunter who later complained that Windham had cost him a good deal of his clientele. I understand, however, that he is now back in business.

In addition, scandals have arisen over presigned I-20 forms, which colleges sign verifying acceptance of a foreign student and which is necessary for the student to obtain a visa and enter the country. A while ago, even some prestigious colleges were sending out recruiters with presigned I-20s. But some headhunters pay little attention to matching students with appropriate colleges. For example, a man who runs a recruiting agency in Florida, primarily to place Florida young people elsewhere in the country, also runs a foreign recruiting service. He says, "I have a double standard that I apply to foreign and domestic students. Before I recruit an American, the student would know a heck of a lot about that institution and vice versa. With a foreign student, it's a blind date—it's an arranged marriage." This recruiter is candid, if nothing else.

In addition to such marketing abuses, colleges have only just begun to consider a number of far-reaching considerations regarding the recruitment of foreign students. One is the question of why colleges seek foreign students. Is it simply to fill classes, or is it to meet a legitimate educational need? I think colleges really ought to confront this issue before they venture into this area. Admitting foreign students is an enormously complicated operation requiring some very specialized skills. It is not something that colleges should be tampering with unless they really are identifying a positive need and not simply making a body-count.

A related question is: On what basis do we displace American students in cases where there are choices to make? This choice probably presents itself most often in high-technology fields, whose curriculums constitute one of the few areas where the United States remains economically competitive. This should continue to be true, and fifteen years from now, higher education may be our major international export. Thus, colleges are increasingly going to find themselves in the position of having a small number of places in specialized fields like physics. On what basis, then, does a college allocate seats to domestic and foreign students? This is a complicated question.

Another important concern has to do with adequate counseling. There was the case of a young woman from Kuwait who, having never been left in a room unchaperoned, arrived at school and found herself in a coed dorm. Fortunately, she was quite mature, and there were no major negative effects, but this is a clear illustration of the need for good counseling services.

Still another question concerning foreign students is whether it is fair to place American students in classrooms with foreigners who may have language problems or inadequate academic backgrounds. A correlate question is: Should we provide foreign students with an American education, or should we adjust our curriculum to meet their needs? A college that attracts large numbers of Middle Eastern students may add a few courses about the economics of petroleum or Middle Eastern politics, because such an institution may need to alter its educational mission to accommodate them. We discovered this in the 1960s, when colleges began taking larger numbers of minority students, a practice that presented no problems while the token group simply conformed to what the college was already doing. When, however, a critical mass of somewhere between 10 and 15 percent was reached, it became clear that there is a substantial group of students with very different needs, and there may be an institutional responsibility to make some adjustments. Of course, if the curriculum is altered, the academic and financial consequences must be ascertained. The area of foreign students comprises half a dozen issues that we have only just begun to think about. As the number of foreign students continues to grow, and as more and more colleges become increasingly dependent on them for income, these issues are going to become even more prominent and troubling.

Major Issues for Action

These categories of ethical abuse in student recruitment suggest several broad issues that deserve attention. First of all, there is a kind of Gresham's law that sets in motion the temptation to sacrifice quality—simply to let standards slide and obtain the requisite number of warm bodies. In the long run, this strategy is counterproductive. Every bit of systematic research that I've seen on this subject suggests that quality is the means of institutional survival.

Second, I question at times the depth of understanding of some college administrators who are pursuing new marketing strategies by hiring consultants. For example, in an interview for an *Atlantic Monthly* article on this subject, a college president told me that his consultant was improving "not only the image but the reality of the institution"— whatever that meant. The admissions director of this college explained that the literature they had developed as part of their marketing strategy "starts out general and/or exciting and moves to more and more detail while connoting personalness throughout, hopefully." And the admissions director at a college in New Jersey explained that its marketing consultant was finding out what certain types of students within the college's drawing area needed in order "to benefitize our school."

A third and related issue is improved professional training of admissions officers. There is a strong advocacy within admissions officers' and counselors' organizations for greater professional recognition and standards. An admissions office is not the place for a recent alumnus to serve as a salesperson for his or her alma mater.

The fourth and final broad issue concerns the fact that, if they begin to act like businesses, colleges are going to be treated like businesses; and if they act like hucksters, they are going to begin to be treated like hucksters, with the likelihood that the federal government will increase its regulation of higher education. There is, after all, a difference between selling education and selling soap. If I buy a car from General Motors, the deal is essentially between General Motors and myself. If the car is a lemon, my quarrel is essentially with General Motors. But in the field of education, public or private, there is a third party with a vested interest—society. Every form of higher education, even in the private sector, is subsidized by public money, and so the public has a stake, as do college students, in what happens in the educational process. The public is fully prepared these days, when it finds that it is being exploited, or misled, or unethically handled, to seek help from government or the courts to redress the grievance.

As we enter the 1980s, there is going to be growing pressure for colleges to slip into quasiethical recruitment practices, and the most effective safeguard against this threat is for colleges themselves to do some self-policing. It has worked so far, with a few exceptions that I have discussed earlier, and it is certainly the preferable route. It is, in fact, the only route if educators and administrators nobly want to maintain that we are not selling soap.

Edward B. Fiske is the Education editor of The New York Times. *In 1978, he received the American Association of University Professors Annual Award for Excellence in Covering Higher Education. Fiske holds master's degrees in political science from Princeton Theological Seminary and Columbia University.*

Racial desegregation still exists on college and university campuses. Administrators and faculty members must promote desegregation efforts.

Moral and Ethical Obligations of Colleges and Universities to Minority Students

Paul B. Zuber

My background and experience qualify me to write with some authority on this subject, even if the fact that I am black does not give me an automatic license to do so. I was born and grew up in a small town in Pennsylvania, and segregation and discrimination have been with me from my first day of life. It mattered not whether it was segregation by statute or by custom; either way, it had a devastating impact. I experienced the segregated schools of Harlem, and when I later charged the City of New York with maintaining racially segregated schools, I knew what I was talking about. My statement was vindicated when I won a court case in 1958 involving black children who were being forced to attend racially segregated schools in New York City. I attended a predominantly white university and knew at first hand the problems a black student faces in that environment. My situation was exacerbated in that, for two and a half years, I was the only black student there. I learned about paternalism and patronizing attitudes and how to diagnose the symptoms of those two diseases. When I returned from military service in World War II, the number of black students at the university had increased to five.

I served in the segregated Army in the South during World War II, and that same segregated Army welcomed my participation on an integrated football team, because the general in command of the base wanted a winning team. The team was housed in the white part of the camp. We practiced together, ate together, and got haircuts from the same barber. At the end of the day, we all retired to two barracks situated next to each other, but the fifty white soldiers went to one barracks and the four black soldiers went to the other: *C'est la difference.* I was called again to serve in the Army during the Korean War. Five years after my first encounter with the military, I was now in the integrated Armed Services by executive order of the President of the United States. I learned that when the decision makers and those in positions of power want something done, it will be done effectively and without delay.

I have spent twelve years in the legal profession and can attest to the fact that bias and bigotry are not the sole property of blue-collar workers or Southern rednecks. I have spent ten years as a professor and director of a graduate program and have learned full well that preconceived notions about blacks' professional capabilities, aspirations, goals, and habits are not the eminent domain of those labor unions that drag their feet when ordered to open up their memberships to minorities. I could go on and on with a litany that could be repeated by my black colleagues a thousand times over.

Many of you are not going to like what I am going to say, but the see-no-evil, hear-no-evil, say-no-evil syndrome is not going to make the bad dream go away, because it is not a dream; it is reality, and it must be dealt with now.

Segregation in Higher Education

I submit that today the predominantly white colleges and universities have become slowly and surely the most segregated and ghettoized of institutions. If we state the cause in legal terms, it is misfeasance and nonfeasance. If we diagnose the symptoms in moral or ethical terms, then the problems are callous indifference; a missionary attitude reminiscent of the Stanley and Livingston era of the nineteenth century; and finally, plain old unadulterated greed.

Two weeks ago, I returned to my alma mater, Brown University, for my daughter's graduation. That is an experience a parent looks forward to, and in my case it was even more special because it was my old university. In a short time, events turned my joy into disgust. Reading the official program of commencement weekend events, I learned that there were going to be two baccalaureate services. The first one was the black baccalaureate service, while the second service was for the entire university and guests. I had just finished spending over forty thousand dollars to get my daughter through Brown's hallowed halls of ivy. The next jolt came when I learned that the black students were having an awards banquet, where they were going to bestow their honors on the oldest living black graduate of Brown; that gentleman was so eminently qualified that the honors should have been bestowed at the general commencement exercises.

My weekend was ruined, and all I wanted now was to seek out the president of the university and get some answers. I finally did; his response was, "What could we do? That's what the black students wanted." My reply was short and blunt: "That's what George Wallace wanted when he stood in the doorway of the University of Alabama blocking a young black woman, but the government didn't let him get away with it, and neither should you." When I posed the same question to the dean of the college, her response was, "You can say what you would do because you are bigger than I am." Here is the crux of the whole problem—patronizing indifference and fear of the consequences if authority is exercised. The students forced things to happen that were illegal, immoral, and unethical. They got away with it because people who had the duty to act and who knew that what was going on was wrong did not have the courage to say, "No—and if you don't like it, pack your bags and go home." This scenario at Brown University has also taken place on hundreds of other college campuses throughout this country.

It has amazed me how the presence of one hundred black and Hispanic students among five thousand students can throw an entire academic community into a state of shock and chaos. Where have these academicians been all their lives? They are completely incapable of dealing with people of other racial groups. Their basic job is to teach, educate, and create an environment conducive to achieving those goals. The black worker in the dean's office should have been there long before the first black and Hispanic students arrived; the Hispanic worker in the admissions office should have been on the staff long before minority students enrolled. Those workers should have been there not only because they were black or Hispanic but also because they were trained and qualified to do the job. Their presence on the administrative staff was essential to the entire student body's receiving a thorough and relevant education. Black and Hispanic faculty members, too, should have been teaching long before colleges decided that the presence of black and Hispanic students warranted courses in Afro-American or Hispanic studies. All along, there have been black and Hispanic academicians available to teach, and they would have enhanced the education of everyone attending America's colleges and universities. They would have stimulated more black and Hispanic students to go on to graduate study, because the students would have seen that it was possible for them to pursue careers in university teaching. But these things did not happen, and we would do well to look at what did happen.

The federal government said, "There will be black and Hispanic students on your campus, or else you don't get money; not only that, we will also cut off funds for other programs." American industry said to the colleges, "The Feds want us to hire more blacks and Hispanics, and if you want our financial support, increase the number of minorities in your graduating class." Private industry followed suit. There then came a directive from on high for a nationwide drive to find black and Hispanic students.

To achieve this goal, misguided souls with little or no exposure to either group created their own minority-student profile, which invariably included the code words *economically and academically disadvantaged,* and they concluded that all of these students were to be found in urban ghettoes and barrios. Nobody bothered to go to the library and gather facts about either group. Since there were no minority workers in the admissions office, the next step was to hire some. Qualifications were forgotten, and the main criterion was that those selected had to look, act, and talk like blacks or Hispanics. The same pattern was used to select personnel for the dean's office. The turnover in these positions is shocking, because people who take these jobs know that they lead nowhere, and they get out as soon as something better turns up.

The circle is now complete, and the students are locked into a segregated pattern from which there is little or no escape. Students who want to be individuals and select their own friends rather than being herded into one corner of the campus find themselves caught in the middle. If there is a special program for minority students on campus, all minority students tend to be identified with the program regardless of their academic standing. Individual achievement and motivation are frustrated, and one soon learns to move with the pack or be isolated. Eventually the group becomes politicized; real and imagined issues and problems become primary, and the original goal of education is lost in the shuffle.

At this point, the administration shrugs its shoulders and decides to let the students do their own thing as long as they avoid putting the university on the front page of the *New York Times* or on the evening news. Ultimately, what results is a classic example of Patrick Moynihan's benign neglect and all its aftereffects. As for the parents of minority students, they discover what has happened only when their sons and daughters arrive home after being dropped for academic reasons or, far worse, just hang around the campus because they are afraid to go home and face the music. One of the spinoffs of this circular pattern is that the students are convinced that they do not need anyone but the group to survive.

How can this happen? Isn't there a structured situation set up to meet the needs of the white students? It died in the 1960s when students took over buildings and backed the faculty and administration up against the wall. In some colleges, the students started to determine who was going to be hired to teach what. They started having major input into curriculum development. If the students did not get their way, they demonstrated or took over a building. After a while, all students had to do was threaten to act, and they got what they wanted. Frustration or mental exhaustion shortened the tenure of college presidents and deans. It is no wonder that black and Hispanic students are emulating the 1960s students' model, with similar results. The real questions are: When does it all end? When will we see the termination of this era of academic anarchy? If the end does not come soon, the state of higher education is going to become worse.

It seems to me that the 1980s will be the decade of decision. The minority programs on the predominantly white college campuses have been failures. It is time to examine what is wrong, and for people in policy making and administrative positions to acknowledge their incompetence and seek help. It is time for administrators to do the jobs they are paid for; if they cannot or will not or are afraid to say "No" when they realize that something is legally, morally, or ethically wrong, then they should pursue other careers. It is time for the faculties to come out of hiding and do their jobs. Teachers have to realize that they can no longer operate in the vacuum of the laboratory or the classroom.

Campus life is an essential part of the educational experience. The "us and them" mentality that has developed over the past twenty years has to disappear. Students have to learn that in our society everyone has to play the game according to the rules, and that those rules are not always going to be of our choosing or have our consent. Parents are going to have to be more diligent in keeping track of what they are getting for the money they spend on their children's education; they are not so trusting when they buy a car or a house.

Finally, the cultural lag between black and Hispanic students and white students is narrowing. No one will be able to deal with one group's problems without affecting the whole campus community. If we cannot achieve some degree of desegregation and racial accommodation on college campuses where select groups of young people are surrounded and influenced by people who are supposed to be intelligent, then God help the rest of this country and its future in world affairs.

Paul B. Zuber holds a law degree from Brooklyn Law School. He has served as counsel to parents groups throughout the country in school desegregation cases, and is currently an associate professor of Law and Urban Affairs and director of Urban-Environmental Studies at Rensselaer Polytechnic Institute.

*Focuses on ethical standards as they relate to
collective actions taken by academic leaders. Ethical
behavior in higher education should be guided by
voluntary efforts of college administrators.*

Self-Regulation: An Approach to Ethical Standards

Elaine El-Khawas

People do the right thing for widely differing reasons. Some take a high-road approach—because of the Judeo-Christian tradition or some other philosophical belief, they think people ought to have ethical standards. Others take a low-road approach and warn that ethical standards are necessary because terrible things will happen if we do not have them; there would be widespread fraud and abuse, perhaps, leading to more government regulation. Mark Twain offered another reason for ethical behavior. He said, "Always do the right thing. It will please some people, but it will astonish the rest."

My specific focus is on ethical standards as they relate to collective actions taken by academic leaders to ensure good practice in institutional policies and procedures. This focus differs from that for individual ethics, which relate to individual decisions, professional standards, and the professional norms and responsibilities a person brings to his or her own work. Institutional and individual ethics are related, of course: Collective agreements about what is ethical and what is not offer a necessary and valuable organizational buttress for individual ethics. In these days of often intense public scrutiny and cynicism regarding the prospects for ethical behavior, we may have a special need for complementary canons of individual and collective ethics.

The American Council of Education (ACE) established its Office on Self-Regulation in June 1978, a time when many people were getting fed up with government regulation. We believed that the academic community itself could deal with many problems and that regulations were neither always necessary nor the only way to deal with problems. Our primary purpose then was to foster greater attention to self-regulation—voluntary actions to address a problem—and to assist other associations, colleges, and individuals who wanted to act on a self-regulatory basis. At the present time, to the extent that we can demonstrate voluntary actions dealing successfully with problems, we also hope to reduce the rate of new governmental encroachment, improve those regulations that we must have, and make it more difficult for new regulations to be developed without prior consultation with the people who are going to be affected.

In our experience, the pressures to develop new standards for ethical or fair practices come from varied sources, including government officials and agencies, students and their parents, journalists, advocacy groups, and the taxpaying public, focusing on a wide variety of real and potential problems. Self-regulation is an approach that stresses the value of voluntary action by members of the academic community to respond to those pressures. The specific nature of the action will vary according to the type of problem that arises and the status of current policies that might deal with it. The response may be national or statewide in scope, or it may involve solutions worked out differently by each college and university. To date, much of our work has resulted in the development of new policy guidelines; nevertheless, other problems might result in advisory or self-study materials for campus use or simply in a call for renewed campus attention to a particular issue.

Examples of Recent Efforts

Tuition and Other Student Charges. ACE issued a national statement on elements of good practice for refunding student charges in late 1979, after extensive review and consultation. The impetus for developing the refund guidelines was federal agency officials expressed concern about collegiate refund policies; on several occasions, they had considered drafting detailed regulations to compel all institutions receiving federal student financial assistance to have fair and equitable refund policies. It was possible that this regulatory approach would have produced a very expensive and onerous set of regulations, and there was some fear that the regulations might mandate pro-rata refunds.

The self-regulation guidelines, however, offer a nonregulatory alternative, which is being acknowledged and accepted by both legislative and federal agency officials. Pending regulations for the Guaranteed Student Loan Program (GSLP), for instance, were revised recently to omit detailed criteria for refund policy and to recognize voluntary guidelines developed by the academic community. In July 1980, Secretary Hufstedler announced that the Department of Education will rely on self-regulation refund policies to cover GSLP requirements and stated that the Department "will continue to rely on the education community for guidance in developing regulations."

The ACE refund guidelines have also gained acceptance in the academic community. Many college and university presidents have indicated that the guidelines are being used for reviewing present policies; typically, only minor changes have been needed to meet the expectations set out in the guidelines. Presidents have also said that the self-regulatory approach alerted them to public concerns and simultaneously signalled to public officials the readiness of academic institutions to review and change policies as necessary.

College Admissions and Recruitment. Another set of guidelines focuses on proper procedures to assure ethical practice in the admission and the recruitment of students. New attention to this topic developed from public concern raised by the news media as well as by the Carnegie Council about the prospects for unduly aggressive recruiting during the coming decade. Because the associations with specific responsibilities in college admissions had already developed an exemplary joint statement on the subject, the ACE Board of Directors endorsed the joint statement and commended it to the attention of all colleges and universities as an effective guide to institutional policy.

These guidelines on college admissions are quite detailed and proscriptive, covering admissions promotion and recruitment, application procedures, financial assistance, advanced standing, and the awarding of credit. They address the continuing tension between shortsighted recruiting aims and the long-term values of ethical conduct. One association has developed regionally organized monitoring systems that review specific complaints related to the guidelines.

Again, campus cooperation has been encouraging. Recently, for instance, we have been informed that two large systems—the State University of New York and the University of Wisconsin—have formally adopted the guidelines. In Wisconsin, a committee review process led to a number of revisions in the original document.

Fair Practice Toward Students. As a voluntary response to both governmental and public concern about fair treatment of students, a model code of fair practice was developed and distributed in 1979 by ACE's Office on Self-Regulation Initiatives. The proposed code outlined principles of fair practice in eight different areas of institutional operations, including publications, record keeping, career counseling, and instructional requirements.

As a follow-up project, a resource guide to campus self-study on fair practice, with emphasis on student services, is being prepared in collaboration with the National Association of Student Personnel Administrators. This project reflects the belief that campus services affecting students should be routinely reviewed to ensure that they follow basic principles of fair and ethical treatment. It also stresses, however, that the translation of those principles into viable policies should be done on a campus-by-campus basis, fitting the principles to the realities of each college's students and circumstances.

Effective Campus Management of Student Aid. A joint association project conducted during 1979 and 1980 has brought pertinent advisory materials to the attention of those college officials who deal with effective management of student aid. A substantial body of government regulation already existed on this topic, but questions remained as to whether colleges and universities would comply with the regulations in a timely and effective manner, and a slow response by academic institutions might well have resulted in even more detailed and exacting regulations. Prompt and positive response, however, would offset the pressure for more regulation. In this case, specific guidelines were not called for; instead, voluntary action was called for to help campuses give adequate attention to financial aid management, and to strengthen and improve financial aid operations. Jointly with other associations, we launched a series of information programs. Several regional workshops for senior administrators were held, and a consultant service has been offered to institutions that want expert external review of their programs. Two major publications have been issued—*Management of Student Aid*, a detailed manual on proper procedures, published by the National Association of College and University Business Officers; and a short companion *Guide for Presidents*, published by ACE in January 1980. Another short advisory document, *Special Policy Issues in Management of Student Aid*, is scheduled for publication in the fall of 1980.

As these examples of self-regulation efforts show, there is likely to be much variation in specific responses to ethical or fair-practice concerns. Certain general principles underlie all of these efforts, however. A fundamental premise is that any statements, voluntary or governmental, about proper behavior ought to be fashioned by people who know what the academic world is like. With the refund guidelines, for instance, the initial drafting involved gathering opinions from dozens of people. Once in draft form, the guidelines were reviewed by literally thousands of people. The draft was discussed by the boards of almost thirty associations, with twenty or thirty college representatives on each board. It was also published for comment in the news magazine of the National Association of College and University Business Officers and was endorsed by ACE's Board of Directors in June 1979.

We follow similar procedures to solicit a wide range of opinion on other issues. We look first to the association(s) with specific responsibility and expertise on each subject. Once a draft statement is developed, we circulate it widely, making use of the numerous information channels available within the associations. If our statements are to be better than government directives, we need wide review to be sure that the final statement accurately reflects a broad range of institutional circumstances.

As should also be clear, guidelines or advisory documents are intended to reflect principles of good administrative practice, but they are flexibly worded, so that the principles can be adapted to the perspective and actual situation of a given college or university. We do not expect colleges to comply with the guidelines, but instead to use them to review existing policies and identify necessary changes.

The obvious question arises of how such guidelines are to be monitored and enforced, and here is where we part company entirely with the regulatory approach. A different mindset is needed to recognize that it is possible and even desirable to develop statements about ethical or fair practice that are not subject to restrictive compliance requirements. Self-regulation stresses voluntary action, including the freedom for each camps, administration to shape its own response to issues of ethical or fair practice. We believe that, on many issues, a voluntary approach can be more effective precisely because it is flexible and offers a greater prospect for new ethical standards or guidelines to fit many different types of circumstances. We are relying on voluntarism as a free market principle—if the guidelines make sense, then people will use them. If some of the guidelines miss the mark or become obsolete over time, we would rather have them fall into disuse. In fact, much generally accepted practice in higher education is based on voluntary adoption by many, many colleges. Campus policies regarding faculty appointments—including promotion, award of tenure, grounds for dismissal, and so forth—reflect common assumptions about fair treatment. Although the policies were developed initially by the American Association of University Professors (AAUP) and other education associations, these policies were in each case voluntarily adopted by colleges and universities. Interinstitutional agreements about accepting transfer credit earned at other colleges is another major example of voluntary adoption of common policies. The corollary to the voluntary use of these and other policies is that, if they no longer make sense, college administrators should be free to change them.

The responsibility for ethical behavior rests fundamentally with each institution. The "self" in self-regulation is the college—the individual institution. The national associations give advice and alert campus administrators to issues that are sensitive, but for questions about what a campus should do and who is responsible for decisions, each institution must rely on its own resources. Depending on the issue, many colleges will develop exemplary procedures of their own without relying on outside advice at all. To be effective, new policies or procedures, whether initiated by externally produced guidelines or not, must be incorporated into the existing fabric of campus life. Institutional commitment and support must exist if any voluntary statement of ethical practice is to have real meaning. It is also true, however, that if an institution finds itself engaged in unethical or unfair practices, it opens itself to reproach by federal agencies, state boards and agencies, accrediting bodies and their member associations, and other concerned agencies and parties. Moreover, detailed civil and criminal procedures already exist as vehicles for dealing with many potential problems of unfair or unethical practice.

Self-Regulation as an Ongoing Process

Aside from recent progress in dealing with specific issues of fair practice, one of the primary accomplishments of self-regulation initiatives is an improved capacity for using voluntary action to address problems. In working on these issues, ACE has helped establish a strong capacity for spurring self-regulatory action—a broadly representative advisory committee charged with identifying areas where self-regulation is warranted, a network of cooperating associations that lend substantive expertise to developing guidelines and policy recommendations, and a widely recognized publication series and dissemination strategy for gaining campus cooperation in policy review. Together, these resources offer a nationally coordinated yet appropriately diverse set of approaches to emerging issues. Various associations and individuals are currently reviewing possible guidelines or other approaches to issues such as:

- Proper college uses of standardized testing
- Quality controls for off-campus programs
- Recruitment of foreign students
- Adequate safeguards for employee records
- Research utilizing student subjects
- Assessing the quality of graduate programs
- Professional standards for student services
- Ethics in college public relations, advancement, and publications
- Handling of academic transcripts of athletes

Other ethical issues are also being dealt with, although not by the drafting of policy guidelines. A committee of lawyers associated with the Center for Constitutional Studies at the University of Notre Dame is drafting a document on how colleges might conduct legal audits. A Ford Foundation grant is supporting a New York-based effort regarding conflict resolution and informal mediation as ways to deal with problems before external intervention becomes necessary. The Society for Values in Higher

Education has been discussing ways for its members and other faculty to play a role in programs for improving the training of accrediting teams.

Sometimes concerns are raised when there is no clear information about the actual problem or possible solutions. In a survey being conducted at this writing, researchers from the University of Michigan are trying to learn how American colleges and universities deal with students' academic grievances. Similarly, a Carnegie Corporation grant has supported an inquiry at the University of Southern California into potential ethical problems regarding outside employment of faculty.

This variety of present activity by associations, special-projects groups, individual researchers, and colleges suggests the myriad ways in which ethical standards are developed. The basic process involves identifying a problem, considering its nature and extent as well as the possible modes of response, and seeking to articulate the critical elements of ethical or good practice applicable to the situation.

Much of this, of course, is not new. In part, we are applying a new title and new terminology to actions taken by associations and individuals who have been doing the right thing all along. Associations have long given attention to developing policy statements or recommendations about new issues; AAUP is one of the best examples we have of a voluntary association developing standards and procedures that have become widely recognized in higher education. The American Council on Education and many other education associations also have long histories of offering recommendations on changing educational policy issues. The American Association of University Administrators has an exemplary statement on the rights and responsibilities of university administrators and supports its statement with an effective mediation service.

What is new, perhaps, is the revitalized commitment to voluntary action as a way of addressing problems affecting higher education. Both on campus and in the national associations, there seems to be an increased readiness to look at tough issues and deal with them, rather than waiting for someone else to take the initiative. In this era of public accountability, waiting has too often led to governmental rules or embarrassing public criticism of higher education. A hopeful prospect of this new commitment to self-regulation is that attention to issues of ethical or fair administrative practice will be possible and effectively conducted.

Campus response is a critical element in this effort's success. To be effective, any of these actions by associations, projects, or individuals require that campus administrators use them or, at the very least, treat them as a warning that new campus issues are being raised or that long-term concerns are reappearing in new forms. Stronger self-regulation in higher education requires campus administrators to deal with problems directly instead of hoping they will go away or that someone else will deal with them. More often than not, fair-practice issues that arise are those on which nobody has direct responsibility. This was the case, for instance, with many of the recent issues falling under the rubric of student consumer protection. It takes a good bit of mental flexibility for a college official to decide on voluntary action as an individual—that is, even though he or she has other high-priority tasks and demands, to take the time to call together the appropriate people and discuss how to approach the issue. That is what a voluntary approach requires: without deadlines or legal requirements, to be willing to address a problem forthrightly, even when the task is not easy and the solutions not readily apparent. Whether on the campus or on the national level, principles of good practice can be developed only by voluntarily setting aside the time it takes to think the issues through.

Elaine El-Khawas, a research sociologist, is the director of the American Council on Education's (ACE) Office of Self-Regulation Initiatives. She formerly served as the director of the Higher Education Panel at ACE and as research sociologist at University Research Corporation. She has published numerous articles and monographs on student consumerism.

*External regulation is inevitable in the
administration of higher education. Administrators
do not themselves deal successfully with ethical issues
because they serve multiple clienteles.*

Academic Chivalry and Professional Responsibility

John M. Farago

The history of government regulation reveals a disturbing pattern: the haves seldom enjoy yielding to the have-nots. Thus, when federalism was an emergent concept, states' rights was the popular counterforce. The Constitution expressed federal prerogatives, but the Bill of Rights sought to restrict their exercise. When emancipation was debated, the counter-argument relied on the property rights of slave holders. When industry was initially regulated, it responded by appealing to freedom of contract. When government began to favor collective bargaining, the right to work emerged as a new, purportedly fundamental, liberty. When segregation was initially attacked, rights in property once again reared their heads. Now, as government has begun to regulate higher education, we hear repeated arguments about incursions into academic freedom. Academe, it seems, bruises every bit as easily as private enterprise. We bristle at making our ivory tower conform to zoning ordinances, OSHA standards, and fair housing requirements.

How may we reconcile these positions? We cannot. Even after millennia of domestication, few horses take naturally to the saddle and the bit. Each colt must still be carefully and patiently trained; each must be broken. External regulation is not pleasant. It is particularly disturbing in academe because it seems to undermine our entire enterprise. The concept

64

of academic freedom assumes that our enterprise is founded on principle—
we are searching for, husbanding, transmitting, and nurturing knowledge.
We are professionals, educators, and scholars, freed from the marketplace
and the polity in order to serve each without necessarily serving ourselves.

Self-Regulation as an Effort to Avoid External Restraints

It is one thing to assert independence from regulation when we are
in the service of others; we have done so for centuries. But when we now do
so in our institutional self-interest, when we argue for administrative as
well as academic freedom, we undercut the very principles on which we
stand. It is a fundamental dilemma: While it may be noble to argue that
academic freedom must permit us the freedom to control the content of our
lectures, it is nevertheless difficult to argue in a principled fashion that
academic freedom also permits us to refuse transcripts to students who have
not paid their bills.

We argue that, as a profession, we must control our own shop, police
our own abuses (El-Khawas, 1976, 1979). Certainly, it is time for teachers to
recognize their professional responsibilities and seek to articulate them.
But affirmative action programs, student recruitment drives, tuition and
financial aid policies, records management systems, and physical access
standards are not part of our academic mantle; they are, instead, the fabric
of our administrative cloak. Thus, in addition to a code of professional
responsibility for educators, a code for professional administrators seems to
offer hope in fending off regulation.

But it has not and will not. In trying to understand why, we must
realize why external regulation is necessary in higher education administration, and why we as ethical scholars and teachers should welcome it,
even as we reject every incursion into our academic prerogatives. The
profession of academic administration is an impossibility. It suffers from
an essential internal contradiction that most of us have not yet grasped. We
seek to act responsibly, although by definition we cannot. Because we
assume that our practices are perfectible, when we observe our necessary
failures we tend to draw one of two conclusions. Either we feel that we need
merely alter our procedures, correct our self-regulatory structure, edit or
rewrite our codes, or we chalk it up, in our cynicism, to the fundamental
weakness of the species. Our goals are aspirational, our behaviors only
human.

Certainly, there is truth to each of these observations, but there is a
more important underlying truth that, once realized, would go a long way
to setting us free: No code, no set of aspirations, however closely followed or
devoutly emulated, can address the fundamental internal conflicts of interest that emerge from our job descriptions.

The inevitability of conflict does not demand the absence of fairness, of course. There is such a thing as a fair fight; we continue to celebrate the spirit of chivalry. At their best, our international treaties seek to emulate this spirit of fairness and to render unacceptable certain forms of combat that, while potentially very effective, seem nevertheless to be unfair. But this chapter argues that our present concerns about fairness in academe are misplaced. We are looking for ways to avoid conflict and are closing our eyes to the inevitability of internal disputes. What we must seek instead are the terms that make the necessary battles fair. And when we look for those terms, we find that the existence of external regulation is not a foe to be obliterated, but a comrade in arms with whom we must occasionally compete.

Anecdotes Involving Ethics

I want to examine, with a minimum of comment, a by no means exhaustive number of anecdotes from my own experience in educational administration. These stories highlight the ways in which all of us often find ourselves responsible for choosing between institutional self-interest and ethical practice. Taken together, they exemplify some of the internal conflicts that our jobs force us to face.

Uses of the LSAT. First, wearing the hat of an admissions director at a selective institution, I observe that the law school admissions process requires all applicants to sit for a three-hour standardized examination, the Law School Admission Test, or LSAT. Additionally, every law school is interested in each applicant's undergraduate record. We have banded together to form the Law School Admission Council—in effect, a trade association—to reap the benefits of orchestrated action on issues of shared concern. One thing we do is have all students submit their transcripts to a centralized summarizing service, the Law School Data Assembly Service, or LSDAS. This saves us the time and effort of analyzing every transcript and converting each into some uniform comparable grading structure. LSDAS does that for us, using a four-point grading scale. But it does much more for us as well. Since it also handles LSAT score reports, it can generate hybrid data. One such datum is the LSAT college mean (LCM), the average LSAT score of all test takers at any particular college over the last several years. By comparing an LSAT score with the applicant's school's LSAT College Mean, we can judge where the applicant stands in the pool of law school applicants from that college. By comparing the LCMs of various colleges, we can derive a general sense of the caliber of the institution, which in turn can aid our assessment of a particular student's academic record. Furthermore, the LSDAS people can tell us about the general shape of the grading curve among law school applicants from most of the colleges in the country simply by aggregating the data already in their files. This further refines our judgment of any particular candidate's credentials.

Finally, the LSDAS service permits us to generate statistical predictions of success in law school. Each year, each school generates an equation that combines the LSAT score and the undergraduate grade point average to yield a particularized prediction of success. The LSDAS uses the school's equation to generate a predicted index for each applicant to the school. That index is also part of the LSDAS report.

Now, a number of interesting ethical questions arise, among them the question of whether manipulating data related to the reputations of various colleges is not some sort of invasion of institutional privacy. But by far the most interesting issue is that law school applicants do not know about anything that LSDAS does beyond the simple summarizing and regularizing of their transcripts. They are not told about the LCM, they do not know about the grade-distribution curves, they are not told about the predicted index.

For the last several years, one segment or another of the Law School Admission Council's committee structure has proposed that applicants be informed of all of this. The Board of Trustees, however, has rejected these recommendations. The tide seems to have turned, though. Recently, a Council memorandum was sent to all law school deans and Council representatives. It reads, in part, "[I]n light of the testing legislation which has been adopted in New York State . . . and because of an overriding interest in the right of each applicant to know precisely what information is being generated about that applicant, the LSAC Board determined in December, 1979, that it was the preferred policy to send applicants copies of the exact document sent to law schools" (p. 25).

This is not an isolated example of the peculiar sort of principled argument which runs, "Because I'm scared of outside regulation, and because I believe there is an overriding principle at stake. . . ." The Council joined with other, similar bodies to endorse a statement of principles that seems to address the applicant fairness issues that testing organizations have been dodging for years. It did so shortly after passage of the New York State truth-in-testing law.

Fair Practices. A second anecdote: The Carnegie Council on Policy Studies in Higher Education and the American Council on Education have called for institutional adoption of various principles of fair practice with respect to students. Valparaiso, like many responsible institutions, has set in motion a committee to study its practices to determine whether they are in fact fair. But when the question of the committee's jurisdiction was raised—when it was asked, that is, whether the committee should address fair practices in general, including all university constituencies, or whether it should limit its inquiry to practices concerning students—the answer came back from the central administration that its task was the latter, more limited one.

The nature of principled investigation is that it must be guided by the principles, not the exigencies, of the situation. A concern for fairness is laudable, but it cannot be cut off by saying, "Yes, we want to be fair to this group, but no, it is less important to be fair to that one." So long as neither this committee nor any other is studying fair practice with respect to faculty, employees, members of the surrounding community, and alumni, the investigation, no matter how beneficial, is not principled.

Freedom to Learn. A pair of anecdotes about incursions into *lernfreiheit*, the oft-abandoned stepchild of academic freedom: New York University engaged in an extensive, if short-lived, institution-wide dialogue about its goals and responsibilities. One question raised was whether the university has the responsibility to provide training in ethical decision making for its students. The dynamics of that particular inquiry were limited, however, to the question of whether all undergraduate students should be required to take some course that would be devoted to ethical inquiry. That recommendation passed. What is unusual is that, while there are many interesting studies concerning training for ethical development, none seems conclusively to validate any particular higher education curriculum. More striking still, the committee steadfastly refused to examine what seems, at least on the surface, to be the most effective technique for teaching moral responsibility—the involvement of students in institutional decision making about issues with ethical implications—investment policy, community relations, and so forth.

A parallel requirement is part and parcel of the recently adopted and much-publicized core curriculum at Harvard College. In spite of the fact that I know of no validated curriculum for teaching writing skills to college students, that curriculum package includes a course requirement in writing. When asked about this, the dean who is primarily responsible for the impetus behind the curriculum neither knew what the curriculum would be nor expressed the belief that such a validated curriculum exists. Of course, it may be argued that the absence of such a pedagogy makes it all the more important to experiment with successful ways of teaching college students to write; that might even justify requiring them to take an experimental course. But unless plans currently exist to engage in that sort of careful course development and evaluation, the core of the core curriculum appears to be an unprincipled affection for academic requirements.

Admissions Statistics. Another tale from the admissions director's perspective: Virtually every law school views itself as highly selective and publicizes this fact by pointing to the ratio of applicants to number of seats in the entering class. That particular figure, however, is rather deceptive, masking the fact that, since each applicant applies to several schools, virtually all schools accept several times as many students as they have available seats. So the more useful figure, ratio of acceptances to applications, is rarely spoken of and hardly ever publicized.

Access to Records. The Buckley Amendment raises several intriguing ethical questions; for example, at Valparaiso a student who refused to sign a Buckley waiver sought to force a faculty member to write a recommendation. The question is whether a faculty member can refuse to write a recommendation for a student who insists on the right to see the recommendation once written. Putting the legal question aside, the ethical question has to do with the nature of the teacher's responsibility. Does the responsibility to evaluate student work stop at the assignment of a grade and the dissemination of transcripts? Or does it extend to a more detailed evaluation, including at least a description of the work that was required, the grading process employed, and the distribution of grades in the course involved? The university chose the former definition.

If we accept the basic premise of the Buckley Amendment—that accountability in student files will lead to less inaccurate or speculative information—how do we address the question of whether an institution should encourage waiver of Buckley rights? How many institutions actively discourage waiver? How difficult would it be to do so? At Valparaiso, we tell students that they may certainly waive their right to see a recommendation, but the committee readers will not know whether they have waived or not. Furthermore, we do not include a waiver form. Fewer than 10 percent of the recommendations that come in include a waiver, and our experience in the two years that we have done this suggests that the quality and apparent honesty of recommendations has improved, not declined.

Finally, the Buckley Amendment permits schools to use data such as first-year grades for test validation purposes, but if such data are released, a notation must be entered in the student's record. Virtually every law school uses first-year grades to validate its prediction equation and does so by sending those grades to the LSDAS for analysis and inclusion in the permanent LSDAS data base. At a Law School Admissions Council meeting, I asked some people whether they included a notation of information release in their students' files. None of the forty or so schools represented could say that they did.

One final note, more a question for future evaluation than an anecdote: The most controversial potential area of current regulation is truth in testing. The dialogue focuses primarily on the questions of whether tests predict accurately and whether they foster cultural bias. Certainly, it is difficult to reject the principle that accuracy should be fostered, but the real ethical question of testing has to do with the criteria we wish to use for selecting students. To what extent are we influenced in our choice of criteria by the fact that a neat, virtually continuous, quantifiable variable (test score, grade-point average, predicted index, and so on) exists and is given to us cost-free (the student pays the freight)? To what extent do we affirmatively select that criterion, and to what extent do we passively accept it by default? How many selective faculties actively discuss the question of selection criteria? These questions are, in essence, the question of whether institutional concerns currently being expressed are ethical ones.

Everyone has stories like these. It is easy to find empirical support for the claim that, at least occasionally, educational administrators act out of institutional, if not personal, self-interest to the detriment of one or more of their clienteles. Does this mean that we are a disreputable lot? Are we all unprincipled and irresponsible? I think not; but I do think the nature of our jobs is such that we cannot avoid this sort of ethical quicksand. The reason for this requires an understanding of how various normative systems interrelate. We must recognize that, contrary to much of our experience, law is not external to ethics or to society. Law is in fact a social response to the perceived ethical needs of a society. This suggests that any understanding of the function of law will require an awareness of the nature of ethics. I shall therefore introduce an oversimplified but, I think, fundamentally clarifying notion of what unites the questions we describe as ethical, and I shall try to unravel the ways in which ethical issues are also yoked to our work as professionals. The experiences already detailed suggest that we do not successfully address ethical issues in our practice as administrators; I shall argue that we do not do so and that, by definition, we cannot. This will ultimately lead my argument back to its origin—that law is not some strange external force imposed on us by a capricious sovereign, an uncaring electorate, or an unwary bureaucracy. It is a slow, evolutionary social process that responds to stimuli in the environment and that seeks to smooth points of stress in the social fabric. As educators, as professionals, and as citizens, we should welcome rather than rebuff such legal intervention.

The Nature of Law

One of the basic paradoxes of our lives is that we are simultaneously autonomous and social, that we seek to live as individuals in a group setting. When we join together, we must take into account the fact that we have individual interests, and that these individual interests may conflict. If we are to stay together and if our union is to remain even remotely stable, we must develop some mechanism for responding to these conflicts (Nozick, 1974).

One such mechanism is the marketplace. We buy, sell, trade, or negotiate our interests, always retaining for ourselves the right to decide whether we wish to engage in any particular transaction. The market, however, is not an alternative to law; indeed, it presupposes the existence of an extensive legal system. Property, for example, is a creation of law. Property interests are not natural or inherent; they are neither more nor less than a means of allocating the scarce resources in which the market trades. Property law begins, therefore, by defining those things it is possible to own and by enforcing some particular initial allocation of those things. It may also come to enforce particular rules governing the transfer of those rights.

For the market to work adequately in a complex social organization, it may also require some mechanism for enforcing agreements and other promises. The marketplace essentially presupposes a need for contract law. And, in a world we do not fully control, we will need to allocate among ourselves the risks involved in our nonmarket transactions. Tort law develops, providing an antecedent understanding of the ways in which we agree to allocate social costs (in much the same way that primitive property law allocates the initial ownership of social assets). Finally, we need to be protected from individuals who choose consciously to repudiate the system, who ignore the property laws, willfully violate our contractual norms, or seek to harm us personally. We need, in short, a criminal law.

We have not exhausted the social origins of law simply by generating the minimal legal system necessary to the functioning of a marketplace. We have social needs as well as personal ones, and our personal interests will often conflict with our social well-being. The most common example of this sort of conflict is the striking paradox of decision theory usually referred to as the prisoner's dilemma.

A crime has been committed. Two persons thought to have collaborated in it are arrested and interrogated separately. The interrogation is simple and straightforward; each prisoner is offered two options. He may remain silent, or he may incriminate his cohort. If he remains silent and is incriminated by his fellow, he will be sentenced to twenty-five years in jail. If he remains silent and is not incriminated himself, he will go free. If he incriminates his colleague, he will be sentenced to a five-year term.

Clearly, if the prisoners could discuss the matter it would be best for them to agree to a pact of silence; each would then go free. But this cannot be the case, and each must assume the worst. Each must assume that the other will talk, and it then becomes a question of minimizing the impact of that behavior. The way to do so is to talk oneself, and so each one will, even though it may well have been the best strategy to remain silent.

Social situations arise in which our interests cannot be determined separately from those of the entire system. Although the prisoner's dilemma seems very artificial, we face such judgments constantly. This is the economic problem of public goods, the particular sorts of social goods that cannot be individuated. National defense is the paradigmatic public good. Arguably, we all have an interest in national defense. But will we all contribute to it voluntarily? If we make the decision rationally, we will consider the fact that, if public defense exists at all, it must be accorded to all of us, whether we pay or not. It is definitionally impossible to individuate national defense. Furthermore, the cost of public defense is so high that any one contribution will not determine whether it is available. Thus, if enough others choose to contribute, I will be defended whether I contribute or not, and if too few others choose to contribute, I will not be defended whether I contribute or not. Granted that my contribution will not have any impact on the benefits I reap, why should I contribute? In practice, the answer has been that, in the absence of an external enforcement mechanism, no rational citizen would contribute for very long, and so, because the market alone fails to yield rational levels of production of public goods, laws must arise to enforce my contribution, either in cash (taxation) or in kind (the military draft).

There is a third source of law beyond that necessary for the establishment of a market and the provision of public goods. It is a fact of life that the market has imperfections; the assumptions on which the market is based are only approximations of reality, and the distance between those assumptions and our practice leads to a variety of ways in which the market fails to serve the functions for which it was adopted. Thus, monopolies and oligopolies develop that can thwart the market as a fair mediator of conflicts among individual interests. We have also seen extensive areas of the law develop forbidding (antitrust) or regulating (utilities law) such market monsters.

Similarly, the market power of individual consumers may be artificially fragmented. The market assumes that each transaction has no effect on all other transactions; no one purchase defines either supply or demand, no one firm sets the price of its goods. This rather accurately captures our experience as consumers, but it is by no means an accurate description of the way in which very large corporate producers operate. It may well be possible, either through trade associations or because of product differentiation, for the producer to deal with all consumers simultaneously, even though each consumer must deal with the producer individually. If the producer acts as if there were only one large transaction taking place, the market will work fairly only if all its customers can aggregate their bargaining power and bargain collectively with the producer. If they cannot do so, their market power will be dissipated, while their adversary's will be concentrated. Accordingly, the market will fail to serve its purpose. Again, we expect to see and do see the law intervening, whether in the form of labor law or consumer protection legislation.

The law is, of course, much more finely woven and complex than this frighteningly oversimplified sketch suggests. The central point, however, is that law develops in response to real social pressures. It is incremental, responsive, paradigmatic; it has no real existence of its own but, rather, serves to operationalize our and, indeed, any social structure. Law is an

72

attempt to manage social traffic, to avoid irremediable bottlenecks that derive from conflicting interests. The legal system is, therefore, natural, if often imperfect; intrinsic, if often intrusive.

Furthermore, our existing legal system evolves excruciatingly slowly and embodies an extremely conservative image of our social needs. It is neither radical nor sudden, revolutionary nor unexpected. Our institutions are relatively unresponsive, our society remarkably heterogeneous. The consensus necessary for the enactment of new law is unusually and, perhaps, disturbingly uncommon.

Persons whom the law affects tend to view it as an outside force. It seems mechanical, imposed, antithetical to consensus. But that perception reflects a willful refusal to grapple with the underlying problem: Law is symptomatic, not pathogenic. It reflects real disease in the body politic, but it is not itself the illness.

The Nature of Ethical Behavior

The tension between social and personal interests generates a need for the sort of normative structure that law provides. A recurrent jurisprudential question asks whether that set of norms is necessarily related to morality (Dworkin, 1977; Hart, 1961). It remains hotly controversial whether the content of law must be tied to any substantive ethical system, but it seems evident that legal and ethical behavior are importantly related to one another, at least conceptually. In order to highlight this family resemblance, I will introduce a deliberately simple definition: Ethical behavior is behavior in which the actor is not motivated by self-interest. Thus, ethical behavior may be motivated by a concern for others or for some ideal. We may do something because we believe it abstractly to be right, or because we wish to further another's interests rather than (and, at least potentially, at the expense of) our own. When we act in this way, we act ethically.

Ethical behavior need not work to our own detriment. In fact, it may well work to our personal advantage. Thus, the prisoner who remains silent out of concern for his partner may do himself harm if his colleague informs on him, but he may also do well for himself if his colleague also remains silent. Neither benefit nor inconvenience is relevant to the actor's motivation, however; that is the core of ethical behavior. It is engaged in without reference to its actual or potential impact on the interests of the actor.

Ethical behavior could vitiate the need for law. Since law arises out of the assumption that we will each seek to further our individual interests, and out of the observation that those interests exist, we might not need a legal system if that initial assumption were controverted. For this to happen, however, two things would be necessary. First, we would all have to agree on a single set of ethical principles. We would have to reach some genuine unanimous consensus about the principles on which we would predicate our behavior. Second, we would then all have to behave ethically. If we all behaved ethically all of the time, we would very probably need no legal system.

Although nothing, in theory, keeps us from fulfilling either of these two requirements, practice strongly suggests that neither of them is likely to be part of our social experience. Our society embraces a diverse and heterogeneous collection of potential values. Indeed, that diversity has for hundreds of years been one of the few values that most of us share. Even here, however, we are by no means unanimous; the emergence of the Moral Majority as a political movement expresses the feelings of a large group of people that ethical diversity is a danger, not a value. And even when we agree that some norm clearly applies to a specific situation, we observe no scarcity of people willing to violate the norm—our prisons, for example, are full. Thus, although we may long for a society of ethical actors, reality delivers us into one in which we must be prepared to enforce at least some of our norms, and the inevitability of enforcement leads inexorably to the establishment of law.

To summarize: Law fills ethical vacuums. When we insist on acting on the basis of self-interest, law is the responsive social mechanism that mediates our conflicts. If we are uncomfortable with any particular law, we should recognize that it expresses an underlying ethical problem and seek to address that problem directly.

The Nature of Professionalism

Professionalism is one extralegal attempt to address ethical questions. It is an institutionalized process of acting on behalf of others, of acting ethically. One solution, therefore, to an ethical vacuum filled by law would be to replace the legal structure with a professional one.

Again, here is a very simple definition: Professionals have clients. Their clients are often helpless, lacking the experience, knowledge, or judgment to make reasoned decisions for themselves. Professionals either decide for their clients or provide their clients with the basis for making decisions themselves.

The definition thus far is too broad. It sweeps in virtually any person who has superior skill or knowledge, even if that skill or knowledge could itself be transmitted or developed through experience. But professionalism requires more; it relates to fields in which the professional must exercise personal judgment on behalf of the client. There are fields in which such professional judgment cannot be avoided. Medical diagnosis, for example, cannot be made sufficiently routine to mechanize the process and eliminate the human judgment of the physician. Similarly, there are fields in which clients simply do not have the capacity to make mature judgments. This is the basis for the teacher's claim to the status of professional. And, precisely because their judgment is necessarily in play, professionals must be trusted. They cannot be held accountable to anyone but themselves. Because reasonable professionals may differ in their judgments, the helpless client has little basis for evaluating them. It is this essential exercise of judgment, this informed playing of hunches, that makes it impossible to replace professionals.

But what makes professionalism inherently untrustworthy? It is simply the fact that the personal interests of the professional may conflict with the interests of the client. To the extent that this is the case, there is a constant temptation to act selfishly. Nor can that temptation be policed from the outside—as a general rule, it will be impossible for nonprofessionals to evaluate the propriety of all but the most egregiously bad professional judgments. Even insiders, other members of the same profession, will have difficulty regulating their peers, for they must recognize a discomfiting dilemma: In instances where judgment must be exercised, there will be many close cases. Procedures for self-regulation must somehow allocate the cost of wrong decision making in such instances. If the cost is allocated to the client, professional standards become conservative and lack bite. But if the cost is allocated to the professional, we will constrain professional judgment and perhaps hamper the delivery of service. The ongoing debate about medical malpractice liability reflects the impossibility of ever finding an acceptable balance between these two possible allocations of risk. For this reason, professionalism is bound up with ethical behavior; the front line of defense against unprofessional behavior must reside with the individual practitioner, and membership in a profession confers a heightened level of responsibility. The responsible person, acting in a professional capacity, must act ethically; professionals, that is, must be guided by their clients' interests and not by their own.

It seems logical, therefore, to expect that professional administrators can and should be expected to act selflessly. Legal intrusion in educational administration seems to challenge the professional competence of educational administrators, to open to question the morality of the incumbents in those jobs. And, since most of us who do administration either teach or have taught, such intrusion seems by extension to challenge the ways in which we fulfill our responsibilities as teachers.

The Paradox of the Professional Administrator

Before examining the specific nature of administration, we should put aside one very important philosophical question, that is, whether an institution or, indeed, anything other than a person can have rights? Can we apply normative assessments to things other than persons? Can a corporation—separate from its human constituents—do good or evil? This sort of problem has profound ramifications for our notions of morality and our entire jurisprudence. It is important to our particular inquiry because it leads to the corollary question of whether a professional can have an institution as a client. Does it ever make moral sense, that is, for a professional to put the interests of an institution ahead of those of a flesh-and-blood human being? I have no answer to the question, although I personally tend to doubt the ethical viability of non-person–based rights. For the time being, however, let us note the question and set it aside.

Having done so, we can take the final step: If we as educational administrators are professionals, we must identify our clientele. Who is the administrator's client? This problem is particularly important to lawyers because of the adversarial nature of their profession. It helps to know whether you are representing the plaintiff or the defendant, but it is far more subtle and important than simply knowing which side you are on. It strikes at the very root of what we mean by professionalism, at the fact that professionals act on behalf of some client's interests. Unless the client can be identified, there can be no basis for judging whether the client's interests have been served.

The issue arises in all professions. Doctors employed by insurance companies report directly to their clients rather than to their patients. A doctor employed by a department store has a confidential relationship with the store rather than with a patient treated while shopping in the store (*Quarles* v. *Sutherland,* 1965). Horror stories about company physicians working for coal mines or sweatshops abound. Similarly, a lawyer working for the government or for corporations must determine who his or her client is. Is it the immediate supervisor, the management, the institution, the shareholders, the electorate? A professional's actions will be determined by how these questions are answered.

Educators have a simple answer to the question. Teachers' clients are students, not as individuals but as role incumbents. To the extent that a faculty member is a teacher, he or she has important professional responsibilities to students, responsibilities that transcend self-interest. For this reason, academic judgments are largely antimajoritarian, nondemocratic. Faculty sovereignty with respect to academic judgment is virtually unchallengeable. Even the courts tread exceedingly lightly on that ground (*Board of Curators of the University of Missouri* v. *Horowitz,* 1978).

But who is the administrator's client? Is it the student? The faculty? The governing board, the institution, the society? It is both tempting and dangerous to say yes to all of these. Having multiple clienteles is like playing chess against yourself. Not only is it difficult even to identify which side you favor, but, worse, knowing the other side's strategy inevitably destroys the very nature of the game. The administrator who has many clienteles with potentially conflicting interests will unavoidably be forced into making impossible decisions among them. The result is confusion and poor representation of all parties. If we look back at the anecdotes with which I began, nothing comes through more clearly than the confusion of purpose that unifies those seemingly disparate stories.

LSDAS reports have been concealed from law school applicants for years. Whom do we serve? Perhaps we serve the law schools, who do not want the inconvenience of having to explain their processes and who are concerned that they may actually have to bargain for the data they receive. Perhaps we serve the administrators who do not want to be burdened with the analytical chore. We certainly do not serve the students, the colleges, or the law faculties. The same sort of analysis applies to the Fair Practices Committee at Valparaiso. Fairness is time-consuming; developing evaluative standards is threatening to those who may be held accountable against them. The institution and its administrators may best be served by arrogating to themselves the broadest discretionary powers. Institutional interests also lead to dubious recruitment practices such as the misleading ratio used by most law schools.

But institutional interests are not the only ones served. Imposition of course requirements without correlative course evaluations serves the faculty's interests, not the students' or the administration's. The same is true of the decision to permit faculty members not to write recommendations for students who do not waive their Buckley rights, and of the decision to use objective measures of academic success as the basis for selecting among applicants to competitive schools.

Even students' interests are served by fair practice committees aimed at developing procedures for student grievances or by application forms such as Valparaiso's, which discourages Buckley waivers, and by the LSAC's begrudging recognition of the right of applicants to know precisely what information is being generated about them.

There are, then, a wide variety of interests served even in this rather constrained group of examples. Other examples might be provided in which administrators have construed their clients as the governing board, the community, or even the society as a whole. There may be cases in which all of these different clients' interests coincide, but there will also be cases where they conflict, and when that happens, the administrator must either choose sides or forsake the mantle of professionalism. If we pick a particular client, we leave everyone else unprotected. If we choose no client, then we are institutional managers offering protection to no one.

It is intriguing that we can observe two very different sorts of administrative structure developing in modern American higher education. In one, the faculty maintains its sovereignty. Administrators are faculty members—educators—first and foremost. The administrators' clients are the faculty. These institutions are bristling under regulations that assert the students' and the community's interests by opening up administrative record keeping, making institutions accessible to the handicapped, to racial minorities, to women, and even by effecting market interventions with respect to such public goods as the availability and distribution of health care.

There is a second sort of administration, one that has been liberated from the faculty. If an institution can be a professional's client, then the institution is the master the administrator serves. Central administration is strong—policy originates separately from any single client population; the machine feeds upon itself. Such institutions are no freer from regulation than faculty-run schools; indeed, since the interests of faculty, like those of students and the community, tend to be unrepresented in these institutions, there is often yet another form of regulation imposed in the form of faculty collective bargaining.

In short, the administrator who wishes to be a responsible professional will have to face difficult questions: Which of the many university constituencies is my client population? Whose interests do I and should I serve? How can I responsibly select one client population if I know that in so choosing I leave others without representation?

The Function of Regulation

Whomever we select as our clients, those whom we do not serve must be represented by someone. Faculty members, like other employers, may be able to bargain collectively, but that solution is a tricky one at best. If the faculty is forced to join together to represent itself in an adversarial negotiating process, its own professional responsibility—to act in the best interests of students—will inevitably be undermined. Tripartite collective bargaining is both rare and fragile. These and others may be excellent educational reasons to maintain faculty autonomy and thereby identify the faculty as the administrator's client.

Students, however, are even less fortunate than faculty. As educational consumers, they lack the relative stability that the faculty possesses. Their association with the institution is of limited duration; at least onefourth exit every year. The current legal wisdom is that applicants to selective institutions are governed by a contract with the institution. But they are given no opportunity to bargain over the terms of that contract, terms that are hardly related to the professional educational judgments faculty members have traditionally and properly reserved for themselves. These terms have to do with price, with due process, with refund policy, with record keeping practices, with consumer information, and with the accessibility and safety of the physical plant. On these matters, students— and, for that matter, nonfaculty employees, community members, applicants, any of the administrator's nonclienteles—have had difficulty pressing their interests.

It is therefore, quite within the bounds of our ethical and professional responsibilities to leave some populations unserved. It is not an indictment of higher education administration to observe that sometimes our actions do not respect the best interests of some members of our communities. But in acknowledging this fact, we must accept a second, correlative truth: We cross an important boundary when we move from actively advocating the clients whose interests we embrace to actively battling our nonclients' right to their own representation. Even the most adversarial legal model assumes that all people will have access to competent counsel; access to advocacy is what makes the system work.

This is a crucial distinction, and a very easy one to miss. It hardly seems logical that we can argue, on the one hand, for administrators to promote their clients' interests while arguing, on the other hand, that administrators cannot seek to further those very same interests by undermining the opposition's right to representation. It is always difficult to understand that there is no inherent conflict between fighting hard and fighting fair.

In part, then, I am urging that we all come to accept that, no matter how sentimentally attached we are to the fiction of collegiality or community, we are necessarily involved in institutions whose many clienteles have potentially conflicting interests. Because that is the case, there will always be internal conflict. It does us little good to seek to eliminate that conflict entirely, but we can and should seek to keep the terms of the combat fair. This is a plea for educational chivalry, for an acceptance of external regulation when such regulation is necessary to express the interests of clients we do not represent ourselves.

One particularly seductive pitfall we must avoid comes when we seek to represent the interests of clients whom we do not serve. Nothing is more hypocritical than the crocodile tears shed by employers defending their employees' right to work or those of the large corporation defending the small businessperson's freedom of contract. This mode of argument is all too familiar to academic administrators. We make this sort of argument as we become more adept at responding to our regulators. We have come to recognize that arguments of blatant self-interest will carry us only a limited distance. If we really want our clients to prevail, we have to disenfranchise the opposition. And so, suddenly, anti-Buckley Amendment and anti–truth-in-testing argumentation is couched in language that seemingly respects the rights and interests of the student clientele. But we cannot honestly and consistently represent those interests, and so we should not express them at all. Rather, if we are to fight fair, we should welcome their proponents into the ring.

Regulation, then, is a way to keep the system honest, a natural response to the cacophony of interests heard in any academic institution. But in spite of the litigative and legalistic model on which I have primarily drawn, the regulative process need not be unpleasantly adversarial; it need not work counter to the forces of community. Legal intervention may seem antithetical to collegiality, because it often serves to patch over crises that collegiality has failed to deal with. It is more difficult and, perhaps, less natural to develop a cooperative conflict resolution technique, but it is by no means impossible. This is one of the lessons to be learned from collective bargaining in the private sector. The continuing relationship between management and labor has led to many situations in which both sides are strong, each side negotiates hard, and all the parties leave the table satisfied.

It is my sense, for example, that there is currently entirely too much due process afforded by educational institutions. Due process requirements do not guarantee a fair fight; they simply make it harder to hide the fouls. When courts come to impose due process on decision making structures, they do so because there is evidence to support concern that one of the parties is manipulating the procedure to mask its manipulation of substance. Because law moves slowly, neither the judiciary nor the legislature is likely to intervene until long after more than enough evidence of impropriety has accumulated. Even then, courts have the disturbing habit of deciding cases on the facts rather than on the law. When the outcome seems fair and the procedures followed seem essentially ethical, it is exceedingly rare that the decision will be overturned.

Thus, much administrative due process imposed on universities out of fear of litigation and unhealthy respect for legalism, rather than out of justice, could easily be replaced by common-sense application of fair practices by administrators. Treat your adversaries as though their position is worthy of respect (treat them, in short, as you wish they would treat you were your positions reversed), leave a paper trail documenting that treatment so that it may ultimately be open to review, and there will be few cases in which, even when dragged into court, you will ultimately lose by reason of improper procedure.

Conclusion: Two Caveats, Two Questions, and Two Pleas

There is a temptation to view less savory academic practices as best met by self-regulation. Self-regulation is, after all, an essential aspect of professionalism. Since we must trust professionals, each profession must be relied upon to regulate itself. But professionalism also calls for a determination of our clientele, and internal professional self-regulation will be effective only with respect to our dealings with clients. Where questionable practices arise with respect to persons whose interests are adverse to those of our clients, there is neither incentive nor logic to self-regulation.

Self-regulation, then, can force us to select among our potential clients, but it will not effectively police transgressions against nonclients. We cannot charge forward in aggressively pursuing our clients' interests while simultaneously seeking to rein ourselves in. As a practical matter, the incongruity of this situation may explain why none of the proposed self-regulatory codes currently in vogue in academe includes any provision for enforcement. The codes remain aspirational, rather than prescriptive, because their appeal lies in our appropriate professional desire to pursue our clients' needs vigorously. It is hardly more appealing to be restrained by one's colleagues than by the legal system.

A second warning echoes one issued at the outset and returns us to the point at which we began: Legal regulation is often annoying. It is costly, both financially and in terms of the time and energy that could seemingly be better spent elsewhere. Bureaucracies develop, expand, and create lives and interests of their own. For the individual litigant—and that means most of us at some point in our professional lives—the structure seems awkward, imposed, impractical, and often unjust. It is, therefore, tempting to reject the system as evil in itself, ignoring the initial stimulus that caused the system to develop in this way.

The legal system is not cost-free, and the rewards we reap from it are far from ideal. The transaction costs of litigation include the defense of frivolous suits, the financial cost of pressing or defending even a valid claim, and the toll the system takes every time it yields an unjust outcome. It is impossible to argue against seeking to improve the system and attempting to decrease the transaction costs. But it is crucial, once again, not to jump from the self-evident observation that this system is not perfect to the hopelessly naive conclusion that we would be better off with no system at all. There is a growing body of criticism addressed to federal and state regulation of higher education, but virtually none of that criticism is constructive. It is all very well to denigrate the medication because it is costly or because it brings with it unpleasant and even serious side effects, but the crucial question is whether some less dangerous or less expensive alternative exists.

If we are to deal with the conflict inherent in the jobs we are asked to do as administrators, we must instead face up to two crucial questions. The first is whether we want to perceive ourselves as professionals. This is a serious crossroad, and we should not be denigrated, whichever path we choose. Our nearness to teachers and teaching makes it difficult to reject the mantle of professionalism, but the vital differences in our roles and responsibilities may make that essential, at least in some institutions. It may in fact be the teachers who recognize that their academic freedom will be jeopardized irreparably if no one is asked simply to mind the store, to manage things efficiently, and to make the necessary resource allocations and balance the conflicting interests of competing populations. We may, that is, be asked to be managers rather than professionals.

But if we select the other path, we must face the second question. That one asks us to identify our clientele. If we really choose to exercise our judgment on behalf of another, we cannot afford not to know who that other is. Too many interests diverge too radically, even on the surface of our institutions; many, many more diverge more subtly just below.

Finally, once we have answered each of these questions, we should heed two distinct pleas. First, we must accept that the system presupposes adequate representation for all parties, both those who are and are not our clients. We are committed not merely to our clientele but to the system itself, and we should welcome such opposing representation. I have suggested why that representation will often take the form of legal regulation, either directly or in support of collective bargaining. Whatever form it takes, however, acceptance of it is part and parcel of our decision to view ourselves as professionals.

Balancing that plea is still another, urging us not to mistake the duty to advocate our clients' interests for a commitment to do so in an adversarial context. We can and should seek nonadversarial models for dispute resolution.

This final desideratum is by no means so simple as it may initially appear. As administrators, we presently either wield or influence virtually all decision making authority in our institutions. Nonadversarial conflict resolution requires us to yield some of the authority we already possess. It is seldom easy to forsake power, and harder still to do so while maintaining an advocacy role. The ability to do so, however, lies at the center of chivalry. What makes a fair fight both exaltingly beautiful and awesomely dangerous is the fact that, by forsaking the opportunity to win unfairly, each of the parties willingly and actively accepts the ultimate risk of loss.

References

Board of Curators of the University of Missouri v. *Horowitz*, 98 S. Ct. 948 (1978).
Dworkin, R. *Taking Rights Seriously.* Cambridge, Mass.: Harvard University Press, 1977.
El-Khawas, E. "New Expectations for Fair Practice." Washington, D.C.: American Council on Education, 1976.
El-Khawas, E. "To Assure Fair Practice Toward Students." *Educational Record,* 1979, *60* (3).
Hart, H.L.A. *The Concept of Law.* Oxford, England: Oxford University Press, 1961.
Nozick, R. *Anarchy, State, and Utopia.* New York: Basic Books, 1974.
Quarles v. *Sutherland*, 389 S.W. 2d 249 (1965).

John Farago is assistant dean and assistant professor in the School of Law at Valparaiso University. He holds a J.D. degree from New York University School of Law, and is pursuing a Ph.D. degree in higher education in New York University School of Education. Farago has published articles on such topics as jurisprudence, education law, and privacy law.

A policy statement setting forth the
responsibilities of professors.

Statement on Professional Ethics

American Association of University Professors

From its inception, the American Association of University Professors has recognized that membership in the academic profession carries with it special responsibilities. The Association has consistently affirmed these responsibilities in major policy statements, providing guidance to the professor in his utterances as a citizen, in the exercise of his responsibilities to students, and in his conduct when resigning from his institution or when undertaking government-sponsored research (1961, 1964a, 1964b, 1966, 1968). The *Statement on Professional Ethics* that follows, necessarily presented in terms of the ideal, sets forth those general standards that serve as a reminder of the variety of obligations assumed by all members of the profession. For the purpose of more detailed guidance, the Association, through its Committee B on Professional Ethics, intends to use from time to time supplemental statements on specific problems.

In the enforcement of ethical standards, the academic profession differs from those of law and medicine, whose associations act to assure the integrity of members engaged in private practice. In the academic profession the individual institution of higher learning provides this assurance and so should normally handle questions concerning propriety of conduct within its own framework by reference to a faculty group. The Association supports such local action and stands ready, through the General Secretary and Committee B, to counsel with any faculty member or administrator concerning questions of professional ethics and to inquire into complaints when local consideration is impossible or inappropriate. If the alleged offense is deemed sufficiently serious to raise the possibility of dismissal, the procedures should be in accordance with the 1940 *Statement of Principles on Academic Freedom and Tenure* and the 1958 *Statement on Procedural Standards in Faculty Dismissal Proceedings.*

The Statement

I. The professor, guided by a deep conviction of the worth and dignity of the advancement of knowledge, recognizes the special responsibilities placed upon him. His primary responsibility to his subject is to seek and to state the truth as he sees it. To this end he devotes his energies to developing and improving his scholarly competence. He accepts the obligation to exercise critical self-discipline and judgment in using, extending, and transmitting knowledge. He practices intellectual honesty. Although he may follow subsidiary interests, these interests must never seriously hamper or compromise his freedom of inquiry.

II. As a teacher, the professor encourages the free pursuit of learning in his students. He holds before them the best scholarly standards of his discipline. He demonstrates respect for the student as an individual, and adheres to his proper role as intellectual guide and counselor. He makes every reasonable effort to foster honest academic conduct and to assure that his evaluation of students reflects their true merit. He respects the confidential nature of the relationship between professor and student. He avoids any exploitation of students for his private advantage and acknowledges significant assistance from them. He protects their academic freedom.

III. As a colleague, the professor has obligations that derive from common membership in the community of scholars. He respects and defends the free inquiry of his associates. In the exchange of criticism and ideas he shows due respect for the opinion of others. He acknowledges his academic debts and strives to be objective in his professional judgment of colleagues. He accepts his share of faculty responsibilities for the governance of his institution.

IV. As a member of his institution, the professor seeks above all to be an effective teacher and scholar. Although he observes the stated regulations of the institution, provided they do not contravene academic freedom, he maintains his right to criticize and seek revision. He determines the amount and character of the work he does outside his institution with due regard to his paramount responsibilities within it. When considering the interruption or termination of his service, he recognizes the effect of his decision upon the program of the institution and gives due notice of his intentions.

V. As a member of his community, the professor has the rights and obligations of any citizen. He measures the urgency of these obligations in the light of his responsibilities to his subject, to his students, to his profession, and to his institution. When he speaks or acts as a private person he avoids creating the impression that he speaks or acts for his college or university. As a citizen engaged in a profession that depends upon freedom for its health and integrity, the professor has a particular obligation to promote conditions of free inquiry and to further public understanding of academic freedom.

References

American Association of University Professors. *Statement on Recruitment and Resignation of Faculty Members.* Washington, D.C.: American Association of University Professors, 1961.

American Association of University Professors. *Committee A Statement on Extra-Mural Utterances* (Clarification of Sec. 1c of the *Statement of Principles on Academic Freedom and Tenure* [1940]). Washington, D.C.: American Association of University Professors, 1964a.

American Association of University Professors. *On Preventing Conflicts of Interest in Government-Sponsored Research.* Washington, D.C.: American Association of University Professors, 1964b.

American Association of University Professors. *Statement on Government of Colleges and Universities.* Washington, D.C.: American Association of University Professors, 1966.

American Association of University Professors. *Joint Statement on Rights and Freedoms of Students.* Washington, D.C.: American Association of University Professors, 1968.

This statement, reprinted from the AAUP Bulletin (Spring 1969), was endorsed by the AAUP's fifty-second annual meeting.

A statement of purpose of academic administrators as
well as their specific rights and responsibilities.

Professional Standards
for Administrators

The American Association of
University Administrators

Just as academic freedom is the special hallmark of institutions of higher
education, so, too, is academic responsibility the correlative of such freedom. Just as freedom to teach, learn, and research are inseparable attributes
of academic freedom for faculty in universities and colleges, so is freedom to
administer an inseparable part of academic freedom for university and
college administrators. The correlative academic responsibility for administrators requires them to exercise academic freedom within the special service functions of higher education and within the objectives of the
institution.

The administrative function in higher education exists to serve the
educational community by facilitating the process of education and by the
creation and maintenance of a milieu conducive to the teaching, learning,
research, and service function of higher education. The exercise of academic
responsibility and academic freedom by administrators requires clearly
understood conditions of employment, parameters of the operation of the
office, career considerations, and personal responsibilities and rights.

A. The Responsibilities of Administrators

1. *Conditions of Employment of the Administrator*
   (a) An Administrator has the responsibility to carry out the duties of the office in such a way as to insure that race, sex, creed, national origin, or age do not enter into the formulation and execution of the policies of the institution.
   (b) An Administrator has the responsibility to carry out the duties of the office as noted in the written statement of the conditions of employment or in the job description published in an official handbook of the institution.

2. *The Administrator—The Operation of the Office*
   (a) An Administrator has the responsibility to direct the utilization of the institution's resources in such a way as to implement the policy set by the governing board, to the extent these resources make possible such implementation.
   (b) An Administrator has the responsibility to utilize the institutional setting in such a way as to further its teaching, learning, research, and service functions.
   (c) An Administrator has the responsibility to participate, according to the nature and authority of the office, in the formulation and implementation of institutional policy.
   (d) An Administrator has the responsibility, according to the nature of the office and within limits set by the charter and governing board, to take appropriate action to develop, allocate, and preserve institutional resources.
   (e) An Administrator has the responsibility to act as official spokesman of the institution only according to the limits of the office held, or by specific delegation.
   (f) An Administrator has the responsibility to create and sustain a milieu on campus such that each person can meet the responsibilities of office without disruption or harassment.

3. *The Administrator—Career Considerations*
   (a) An Administrator has the responsibility to give due consideration to candidates within the institution for jobs that may become available.
   (b) An Administrator has the responsibility to improve professional and personal performance by attendance at appropriate meetings and by participation in the regular development programs of the institution, such as sabbaticals and leaves of absence.
   (c) An Administrator has the responsibility to be just, and to avoid arbitrary or capricious actions regarding subordinates, especially in decisions affecting continuation or termination of office.
   (d) An Administrator has the responsibility to participate in and assume responsibility for the regular and formal evaluation process of those

under the Administrator's jurisdiction and to communicate to them in a timely fashion the results of the evaluation.

(e) An Administrator has the responsibility to draw up and make available a written statement regarding the performance evaluation and the circumstances regarding the departure from the institution of those under the Administrator's supervision. The statement should be released only with the approval of the person who has departed from the institution.

(f) An Administrator has the responsibility to seek actively new employment for a staff worker under the Administrator's jurisdiction whose employment was terminated solely due to a reallocation of resources.

4. *Personal Responsibilities of the Administrator*

(a) An Administrator has the responsibility, when speaking as a private person regarding campus issues or issues that have no connection with the campus, to make clear that the Administrator is speaking in that capacity and not as a representative of the institution.

(b) An Administrator has the responsibility to respect the right of privacy of others, particularly with regard to personal circumstances, including but not limited to financial information, religious beliefs, and political associations.

(c) An Administrator has the responsibility to make clear to a subordinate that participation in associations and support of causes is undertaken as a private person and not as a representative of the institution, and that the only restraints are those imposed by the job description.

(d) An Administrator has the responsibility to provide subordinates with the right of due process and to encourage and participate in the codification and promulgation of the institution's code of academic due process.

B. The Rights of Administrators

1. *Conditions of Employment of the Administrator*

(a) An applicant for an appointment as an Administrator has a right to consideration for employment without regard to race, sex, creed, national origin, or age.

(b) An Administrator has a right to a written statement of the conditions of employment, including, but not limited to, statements on salary and fringe benefits, term of office, process of review, date of notification of action regarding renewal or continuance, and responsibilities of the position.

2. *The Administrator—The Operation of the Office*

(a) An Administrator has the right to resources consistent with the responsibility to implement policies set by the institution's governing board.

(b) An Administrator has the right to a supportive institutional setting for the proper operation of the office held.

(c) An Administrator has the right to adequate authority to the extent necessary to meet the responsibilities of the office.

(d) An Administrator has the right to participate, according to the nature and authority of the office and within the limitations of the area of responsibility, in the formulation and implementation of institutional policy.

(e) An Administrator, according to the nature of the office and within limits set by the charter and governing board, has the right to take appropriate action to develop, allocate, and preserve all resources of the institution, material and human.

(f) An Administrator has the right to act as official spokesman for the institution only according to the limits of the office held, or by specific delegation.

(g) An Administrator has the right to meet the responsibilities of the office held without disruption or harassment.

3. *The Administrator—Career Considerations*

(a) An Administrator has the right to be considered for career advancement opportunities within the institution.

(b) An Administrator has the right to support for efforts undertaken to enhance personal growth and development by such means as attendance at professional meetings and by sharing in any regular staff development programs of the institution, such as sabbaticals and leaves of absence.

(c) An Administrator has the right to be free from arbitrary or capricious action on the part of the institution's administration or governing board, especially in those decisions affecting continuation or termination of office.

(d) An Administrator has the right, under conditions established by the institution's board, to regular and formal evaluation of job performance, to participation in the evaluation process, and to receipt of timely knowledge of the results of such evaluation.

(e) An Administrator has the right, when leaving an institution, to obtain written statements from the institution reflecting clearly and accurately job performance evaluation and the circumstances regarding departure. Such statements should be available for release upon request of the Administrator.

(f) An Administrator has the right, in cases of termination of employment due to a reallocation of resources, to be assisted actively by the institution in seeking new employment.

4. *Personal Freedom of the Administrator*

    (a) An Administrator has the right to speak publicly and to express personal opinions regarding campus issues or issues that have no connection with the campus.

    (b) An Administrator has the right to privacy with regard to personal circumstances, including, but not limited to, financial information, religious beliefs, and political associations.

    (c) An Administrator has the right to participate in associations of his or her choice and to support causes, subject only to the constraints imposed by institutional responsibilities or conflict of interest considerations.

    (d) An Administrator has a right to due process. Such due process procedures should be codified, promulgated in writing, and communicated to the Administrator prior to appointment.

*This statement was reprinted from the AAUP
Bulletin (Spring 1969).*

The editors offer a summary of issues as well as directions to additional sources of information.

Conclusions and Further Readings

M. Carlota Baca
Ronald H. Stein

We would be remiss if we concluded this sourcebook without at least briefly expounding on a fact that a number of the authors have already alluded to—the role of extra-university organizations or agencies in setting the ethical standards for higher education.

Sources of Support for Standards

First, the American Association of University Professors (AAUP) and the American Association of University Administrators (AAUA) have played a significant role in establishing professional standards for college and university faculty and administrators. AAUA's role in ethics was formalized in 1975 with the adoption of the *Professional Standards for Administrators* (reprinted in this volume). This statement is more inclusive than the AAUP statement on Professional Ethics, reproduced earlier, and also includes within its purview matters similar to those found in AAUP's 1976 statement, *Recommended Institutional Regulations on Academic Freedom and Tenure.*

Second, regional accrediting agencies have played a substantial role in promulgating and enforcing professional ethics in higher education.

They have established codes of ethics that govern the relationship between themselves and the institutions they accredit as well as governing the behavior of their members who participate in the accrediting process. For the most part, these accrediting bodies have developed procedures to ensure that the standards of professional ethics are enforced. One view of the importance of their role is set forth by James A. Philips (in a personal communication), executive director of the Association of Independent Colleges and Schools Accrediting Commission, who writes: "The premise of ethics, both in educational programs and business practices of our schools, is basic to the philosophy of our association. The total accrediting process is undergirded with the premise of integrity and ethical practices. Many member institutions of AICS have had their accreditation withdrawn when their standards of quality are diminished below the level of compliance with accrediting standards. In some cases, non-adherence to ethical practices has led to the diminution of quality resulting in the loss of accreditation."

Third, besides AAUP and AAUA, a number of other professional organizations representing subsets of college and university professionals have adopted ethical standards for their members. These include the Council on Social Work Education, the National Association of College and University Business Officers, the American Association of Collegiate Registrars and Admissions Officers, and the Association of Physical Plant Administrators of Universities and Colleges. Recently, a number of these organizations worked together on a common ethical problem with laudable results—standards governing the conduct of admitting and recruiting college students. Because the problem cuts across both associational and institutional lines, four national associations—the American Association of Collegiate Registrars and Admissions Officers, the National Association of College Admissions Counselors, the College Entrance Examination Board, and the National Association of Secondary School Principals—banded together to promulgate a set of ethical standards. This self-regulation initiative, "Joint Statements on Principles of Good Practices in College Admission and Recruitment," covers four main areas: admission, promotion, and recruitment; application procedures; financial assistance; and advanced-standing students and the awarding of credit. It sets forth not only the ethical obligations of colleges and universities but also the related ethical obligations of high schools and community agencies.

Fourth, state governments have played a role in two areas in defining ethical conduct for institutions of higher education. Since state university employees are public employees, their conduct is governed by the codes of ethics that states have adopted for their elected officials and public employees. The states are also recognized to have extensive power over both public and private education. This power is manifested in governing boards such as New York's Board of Regents and in state officials such as commissioners of education. An example of the role these boards and officials can play in setting standards of ethical conduct for higher education can be seen in a recent action by Gordon Ambach, the New York State commissioner of education. Confronted with the problem of how to guarantee ethical behavior by colleges and universities in their advertising and recruiting efforts, he established an advisory group on postsecondary regulations. This group developed a code of ethics that provided for truth in advertising and recruiting. The code, which has been accepted by all segments of New York State's higher education community, requires that statements be "clear, current, accurate, and factual." Any endorsement must be without compensation and must identify the author and his or her qualifications. The students who are recruited must not be promised employment after graduation unless the employment has been actually arranged. Financial aid should not be used as the sole enrollment incentive, nor should recruiters be paid according to the number of students they enroll.

Finally, it should be briefly mentioned that the federal government has played a significant role in promulgating laws and regulations designed to regulate the ethical behavior of institutions of higher education. The role the government sees for itself and its responsibility in this area have already been addressed in this volume by Elaine El-Khawas, John Farago, and Susan Vance.

In closing, we have attempted to show that ethics in higher education is an important and emerging field. Prominent authors are now turning their attention to identifying the ethical dilemmas facing institutions of higher education. Many of these authors are recommending novel approaches, strategies, and solutions, and some of them are listed in the bibliographic sources that follow.

Sources of Further Information

American Association of Collegiate Registrars and Admissions Officers, College Board, National Association of College Admissions Counselors, or National Association of Secondary School Principals. *Joint Statement on Principles of Good Practice in College Admissions and Recruitment.* 1979.
American Personnel and Guidance Association. *Ethical Standards.* Washington, D.C.: American Personnel and Guidance Association, 1974.
Bernard, M. L., and Bernard, J. L. "Institutional Responses to the Suicidal Student: Ethical and Legal Considerations." *Journal of College Student Personnel,* March 1980, pp. 109–113.
Bok, S. *Lying: Moral Choice in Public and Private Life.* New York: Pantheon Books, 1978.
Carnegie Council on Policy Studies in Higher Education. *Fair Practices in Higher Education: Rights and Responsibilities of Students and Their Colleges in a Period of Intensified Competition for Enrollments.* San Francisco: Jossey-Bass, 1979.

El-Khawas, E. "Toward a Statement of Fair Practice." *AGB Reports*, September-October 1978, pp. 37–40.

El-Khawas, E. "Putting the Student Consumer Issue in Perspective." *Educational Record*, Summer 1979, pp. 282–294.

El-Khawas, E. "To Assure Fair Practice Toward Students." *Educational Record*, 1979, *60* (3), 282–294.

Goddard, W. "Suggested Advertising Guidelines for Educational Institutions." Washington, D.C.: National Association of Trade and Technical Schools, 1974.

Kaplin, W. A. *The Law of Higher Education: Legal Implications of Administrative Decision Making.* San Francisco: Jossey-Bass, 1978.

Mikos, E. "Ethical Aspects of Administrative Action: Implications for Research and Preparation." *Administrators' Notebook*, 1977–1978, *26* (5), 1–4.

Plante, P. R., and Raskin, B. L. "From Here to Integrity." *Journal of the National Association of College Admissions Counselors*, February 1980, pp. 12–15.

Scully, M. G. "Can Colleges Keep Their Integrity as Times Get Harder?" *Chronicle of Higher Education*, April 9, 1979, pp. 3–4.

Scully, M. G. "Carnegie Council Detects Ethical Decay in Higher Education, Sees It Spreading." *Chronicle of Higher Education*, April 23, 1979, p. 1.

Stude, E. W., and McKelvey, J. "Ethics and the Law: Friend or Foe?" *Personnel and Guidance Journal*, May 1979, pp. 453–456.

M. Carlota Baca is an assistant to the president at the State University of New York at Buffalo and director of the University's Honors Program. She is a former American Council on Education Fellow and recently served as program co-chairperson of AAUA's National Assembly IX.

Ronald H. Stein is an assistant to the president at the State University of New York at Buffalo. He was program co-chairperson for the AAUA National Assembly IX, and is consulting editor for New Directions for Higher Education. *Stein has published articles on the topics of the impact of federal regulations on higher education and law and higher education.*

Index

A

Academic freedom: ethical issues in, 2, 9–11; and natural law, 9–10
Access to records, issue of, 68
Accountability, of faculty, 18–19, 22, 23, 24
Accrediting agencies, and professional ethics, 93–94
Administrators: clients of, 75–81; in conflict with faculty, 16–17; efficiency of, 42; ethical issues for, 65–69; ethical responsibility of, 1–13; examples of conflicts with faculty by, 22–26; faculty view of, 19–20; professional responsibility of, 63–82; professional standards for, 87–91; as professionals, 74–77, 80; secular view by, 20–22
Admissions: self-regulation of, 57; statistics on, issue of, 67–68; training for work in, 47
Affirmative action: administration and faculty views of, 23; ethical issues of, 11
Ambach, G., 95
American Association of Collegiate Registrars and Admissions Officers, 94, 95
American Association of University Administrators (AAUA), viii, ix, 61, 87–91, 93
American Association of University Professors (AAUP), viii, 59, 61, 83–85, 93
American Council on Education (ACE), 57, 58, 61, 66; Office of Self-Regulation Initiatives of, 56, 57
American Personnel and Guidance Association, 95
Aquinas, T., 6
Aristotle, 6, 7
Association of American Colleges, Project on the Status and Education of Women of, 39

Association of Independent Colleges and Schools Accrediting Commission (AICS), 94
Association of Physical Plant Administrators of Universities and Colleges, 94

B

Baca, M. C., vii–ix, 93–96
Benson, D., 38
Bernard, J. L., 95
Bernard, M. L., 95
Bloustein, E. J., 39
Board of Curators of the University of Missouri v. *Horowitz*, and faculty sovereignty, 75, 81
Bodenheimer, E., 4, 12
Bok, S., 95
Bowdoin College, prospectus of, 42
Brown University, segregation at, 50–51
Buckley Amendment, 68, 76, 78

C

California, University of, at Berkeley, reorganization attempt at, 21
Cannon v. *The University of Chicago, et al.*, and institutional accountability, 37, 40
Carnegie Corporation, 61
Carnegie Council on Policy Studies in Higher Education, 57, 66, 95
Chambers, C. M., vii, ix, 1–13
Charitable enterprises, ethical issues of, 2–3, 11–12
Civil Rights Act of 1964, Title VII of, and sexual harassment, 29, 33–34, 35–36
Clark, S., 38
Cleveland, H., 19, 27
Clients: of administrators, 75–81; and professionalism, 73–74
College Entrance Examination Board, 94, 95

Contracts: capacities of parties to, 7, 8; and ethical behavior, 6–11
Council on Postsecondary Accreditation, ix
Council on Social Work Education, 94
Court decisions: on clients of professionals, 75; on *in loco parentis*, 7; on sexual harassment, 35, 37

D

Dodderidge, E., 31–32, 40
Dworkin, R., 72, 81

E

Educational Amendments of 1972, Title IX of, and sexual harassment, 29, 34, 35–36
El-Khawas, E. H., viii, 55–62, 64, 81, 95, 96
Equal Employment Opportunity Commission (EEOC), viii, 33–34
Equal opportunity, ethical issues of, 11, 49–53
Ethics: for administrators, 1–13, 65–69; background of, 1, 5; development of perceptions of, 8, 67; interest in, vii; and law, 3–7, 69, 72–73; and minority students, 49–53; nature of, 72–73; need for, 2; professional, 83–91; of professional responsibility, 63–82; of recruitment, 41–48; and self-regulation, 55–62; sources of information on, 95–96; sources of principles of, 4–6; sources of support for, 93–95
Etzioni, A., 16–17, 27

F

Faculty: accountability of, 18–19, 22, 23, 24; administrators in conflict with, 16–17, 22–26; sacerdotal view by, 17–20
Fair practices: and administrators, 66–67; toward students, self-regulation of, 57–58
Farago, J. M., viii, 63–82, 95
Farley, L., 39
Federal government, and professional ethics, 95

Feldman, D., 15*n*
Financial aid, self-regulation of, 58
Fiorella, M., ix
Fiske, E. B., viii, 41–48
Ford Foundation, 60
Freehof, S., 3, 12

G

Goddard, W., 96
Gott v. *Berea College*, 7
Guaranteed Student Loan Program (GSLP), and self-regulation, 56–57

H

Hart, H.L.A., 72, 81
Harvard College, core curriculum at, 42, 67
Higher education: and institutional liability for sexual harassment, 34–35; sacerdotal view of, 17–20; secular view of, 20–22; segregation of, 50–53
Hobbes, T., 9, 12
Hollander, P. A., viii, ix
Hufstedler, S., 57

I

In loco parentis, ethical issues in, 2, 7–8
Indiana University, and foreign students, 45

J

Jellinek, G., 3, 12
Johnson v. *University of Pittsburgh*, and insufficient understanding of institution, 37, 40

K

Kaplin, W. A., 96
Kentucky, and *in loco parentis*, 7
Kohlberg, L., 8, 12
Kristol, I., 18, 21, 27
Kunda v. *Muhlenberg College*, and institutional accountability, 37, 40

L

Law: concept of, 3; and ethics, 3–7, 69, 72–73; and marketplace, 69–70, 71; nature of, 69–72; sources of, 69–71

New Directions Quarterly Sourcebooks

New Directions for Higher Education is one of several distinct series of quarterly sourcebooks published by Jossey-Bass. The sourcebooks in each series are designed to serve both as *convenient compendiums* of the latest knowledge and practical experience on their topics and as *long-life reference tools*.

One-year, four-sourcebook subscriptions for each series cost $18 for individuals (when paid by personal check) and $30 for institutions, libraries, and agencies. Single copies of earlier sourcebooks are available at $6.95 each *prepaid* (or $7.95 each when *billed*).

A complete listing is given below of current and past sourcebooks in the *New Directions for Higher Education* series. The titles and editors-in-chief of the other series are also listed. To subscribe, or to receive further information, write: New Directions Subscriptions, Jossey-Bass Inc., Publishers, 433 California Street, San Francisco, California 94104.

New Directions for Higher Education
JB Lon Hefferlin, Editor-in-Chief

1973: 1. *Facilitating Faculty Development,* Mervin Freedman
       2. *Strategies for Budgeting,* George Kaludis
       3. *Services for Students,* Joseph Katz
       4. *Evaluating Learning and Teaching,* Robert Pace
1974: 5. *Encountering the Unionized University,* Jack Schuster
       6. *Implementing Field Experience Education,* Jack Duley
       7. *Avoiding Conflict in Faculty Personnel Practices,* Richard Peairs
       8. *Improving Statewide Planning,* James Wattenbarger, Louis Bender
1975: 9. *Planning the Future of the Undergraduate College,* Donald Trites
    10. *Individualizing Education by Learning Contracts,* Neal Berte
    11. *Meeting Women's New Educational Needs,* Clare Rose
    12. *Strategies for Significant Survival,* Clifford Stewart, Thomas Harvey
1976: 13. *Promoting Consumer Protection for Students,* Joan Stark
    14. *Expanding Recurrent and Nonformal Education,* David Harman
    15. *A Comprehensive Approach to Institutional Development,* William Bergquist, William Shoemaker
    16 *Improving Educational Outcomes,* Oscar Lenning

New Directions for Child Development
William Damon, Editor-in-Chief

New Directions for College Learning Assistance
Kurt V. Lauridsen, Editor-in-Chief

New Directions for Community Colleges
Arthur M. Cohen, Editor-in-Chief
Florence B. Brawer, Associate Editor

New Directions for Continuing Education
Alan B. Knox, Editor-in-Chief

New Directions for Exceptional Children
James J. Gallagher, Editor-in-Chief